Small-Scale Game Rearing

- SMALL~SCALE -
GAME REARING

J.C. Jeremy Hobson

The Crowood Press

First published in 1988 by
The Crowood Press Ltd
Gipsy Lane, Swindon
Wiltshire SN2 6DQ

This impression 1991

British Library Cataloguing in Publication Data

Hobson, J. C. Jeremy
Small-scale game rearing.
1. Game protection – Great Britain
I. Title
639.9'5'0941   SK505

ISBN 1 85223 018 5

Typeset by Qualitext Typesetting, Abingdon, Oxon
Printed in Great Britain by Redwood Press Ltd, Melksham, Wiltshire

Contents

Acknowledgements

First and foremost, thanks to Val Porter, without whose help and expertise none of my books would have ever seen the light of day. Secondly, to Mr James and Richard Drew who have advised on the current renting procedures.

Gina Arnold has provided most of the photographs, but thanks must also go to Richard Hedger who took the photographs on pages 16 and 79 and has helped me for several years by picking up, keeping records for the game book and being there with an encouraging word at the beginning of each shooting season. Nick Brown was kind enough to provide the photographs on pages 20 and 21 and Geoff Burch provided that on page 46.

No keeper can carry out his duties without the knowledge gained from his original head keeper or from conversations between contemporary keepering colleagues and so I include both dedications and acknowledgements to all of the many keepers it has been my pleasure to meet during the course of my career.

Introduction

No would-be gamekeeper has ever been tempted into the profession by the thought of making his fortune. Despite this fact, when a keepering job is advertised in the sporting press, the advertiser is likely to be inundated with replies. At least two-thirds will be immediately discarded because they are either after a free cottage or have no knowledge whatsoever of what the job really entails.

The job may also appeal to shooting enthusiasts who would like the life-style but realise that a keepering life could not provide them with the wherewithal for a comfortable existence. There is, however, no reason why enthusiasts, or those who have no knowledge but are keen to learn, should miss out on the fun to be had from keepering.

This was not always the case and, until comparatively recently, large keepered estates monopolised any shooting available – there was very little opportunity for a few friends to get together and create a shoot of their own. Even tenant farmers were not allowed to carry a gun over ground which they rented; indeed, their tenancy agreement would have precluded any sporting rights.

Thankfully, such situations rarely exist now, and it is possible for ordinary shooting people with an interest in keepering to combine both shooting and keepering with their usual life-style. Since the break-up and sale of many of those large estates, much worthwhile shooting has been built up from nothing more than a few hedges, and with very little financial outlay, by people of all ages, all walks of life and most income groups. This type of shooting cannot rely on the services of a full-time gamekeeper. For one thing, the costs involved would be prohibitive; for another, the terrain and acreage available would not warrant such a luxury.

For the individual's sport to be a success, it is necessary for the small-time shooter (either on his own or by forming a syndicate) to involve himself with the rearing, releasing and feeding of the pheasants which are to form the nucleus of this sport. Without all-year-round attention, the shoot will never be a success; those who feel that shooting merely consists of standing forward whilst a team of beaters drive the wood towards them need read no further.

Fortunately, increasing numbers of shooting enthusiasts are beginning to understand just what is involved from month to month if they are to enjoy a successful shooting season, and are discovering the attractions of gamekeeping on a small scale. The rearing of gamebirds often gives them as much, if not more, enjoyment than the actual shooting day, and it is to enhance this enjoyment and to help solve some of the inevitable problems that this book has been written.

1

Preparation, Predator and Pest Control

Preparation

One of the new gamekeeper's first requirements is to determine what sort of shoot is wanted and how much time can be devoted to its development. A lot will depend on what type of ground can be rented or borrowed, from what source, and under what arrangement (factors which will be enlarged

Catching next year's laying stock. Notice that the catcher is situated next to a release pen in order to pick up birds returning to the roost. As the pheasants peck at the maize through the funnels, they will walk in quietly, without realising that they are caught.

9

Never attempt to grab hold of a pheasant by its tail; it comes out very easily as part of its defence mechanism against predators.

upon in Chapter 2). It is, however, a good idea to assess how much time and money is available before looking for some suitable ground.

Although it will never be possible for the part-time amateur keeper to devote the same amount of time to his game rearing as the professional, there is no reason why this fact should put off anyone considering his own shoot. In fact, the amateur could be in a better position than his professional counterpart, as his shooting acreage is likely to be smaller. So too will be the number of poults in his charge. In order to earn his keep, the professional will be literally rushed off his feet during the busy periods of rearing and releasing, unlike the part-timer who, dealing with small numbers, can treat his birds more like pets and probably suffer less in the way of losses.

Because of the time available, some of the duties carried out by the professional gamekeeper will have to be forfeited when game rearing on a small scale. For example, the catching up of laying birds is not likely to be a worthwhile operation on the small shoot because of the difficulties involved in catching up sufficient numbers of hens to fill a laying pen.

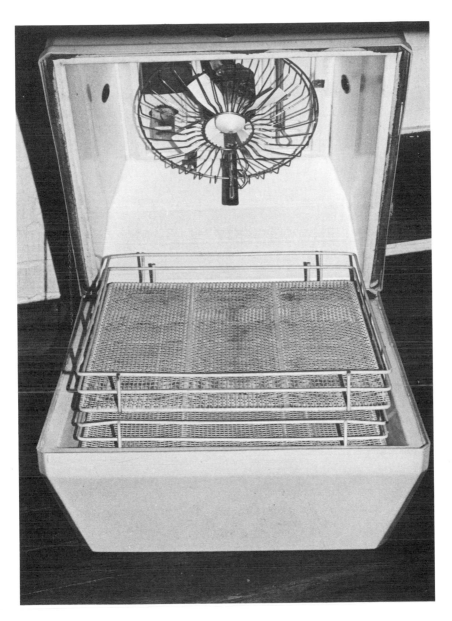

A cheap, easily obtainable incubator, suitable for around 200 pheasant eggs.

Acquiring Stock

It is assumed throughout this book that you will not be releasing any more than 500 pheasants. Initially, the stock will probably have to be obtained from a game farm, either as day-olds or as six-week-old poults. What happens after this is in your hands, but it is safe to say that, from the original stock released, about 300 will be shot. Another 100 will never have seen the start of the shooting season, either falling foul of predators soon after their release, or succumbing to disease. This leaves (at the end of the first season) a nominal figure of around 100. Of these , 50 will be hens. If you are clever enough to catch up all 50, you can expect to pick up 350 eggs in one week during their optimum laying period (May–June). A 75 per cent hatch will leave the operator with 225 chicks from one setting in an average-sized incubator.

At first glance it may seem a good idea to catch up and hatch 225 chicks which, it must be admitted, is the ideal number for a small rearing shed, but the matter does not end here and requires some further consideration. For argument's sake, say that the first lot of eggs is set in the incubator on Friday 1 May. It takes 24 days to hatch a pheasant chick, so the first batch will be appearing on Sunday 24 May, and will fill one brooder unit.

Hens will still be laying well at this time but it will be another week before suffiicient eggs have been collected to fill the incubator for a second time. This second hatch should occur on 23 June. Assuming a further 75 per cent hatch, this makes a total of 450 day-old chicks. Unfortunately, no rearer, even if he spends all his time seeing to the chicks, will bring all of these birds to maturity and so, just to be on the safe side, a third setting will be required in order to be sure of releasing 500 poults.

By this time, the adult birds will be going off the lay and it may take two weeks to collect enough eggs to fill the incubator. These eggs will be set on 8 July, will hatch during the first week in August. You are now, no doubt, beginning to see the problem. Who has ever heard of September-released pheasants, and who can wait until nearly Christmas before beginning shooting?

Predator Control

One aspect of the professional keeper's duties which cannot be ignored by the amateur is that of predator control. It matters little whether you intend to release poults annually or rely on wild bird stocks; one of your first needs is to give the gamebird the best possible chance of survival. The best way of doing this is to keep the population of known enemies to a minimum. Research by the Game Conservancy has shown that as many as

35 per cent of known nests in a given area can be destroyed by predators. Members of the crow family destroy nearly 30 per cent of this total, with the remaining 5 per cent being killed by foxes, rats and stoats. Faced with this evidence, building up a small shoot must begin in the early part of the year with vermin control in its varied forms.

When the DIY shoot is being carried out on property other than your own, it is often necessary to control vermin for the farmer's benefit as well as that of the shoot. It may, in fact, form part of a written agreement signed when first negotiating rent and conditions, so it would be foolish to neglect this aspect and risk losing the land.

Trapping

A good general-purpose trap is the Fenn Mk 4. In it, it is possible to catch stoats, weasels, rats, squirrels and young rabbits, and it has been known to hold successfully as large an animal as a mink. With the exception of the

A partially completed Fenn trap. Another turf needs to be added; the shallow run-ins in the foreground will encourage stoats and weasels. The two hazel sticks at the opening prevent injury to dogs or gamebirds.

last animal, provided that the trap has been correctly set it should kill its victim instantly and live up to its reputation of being humane.

Before even setting a trap it is necessary to know a little of the predators' habits and to be able to detect signs of their presence. Apart from perhaps catching a glimpse of a stoat or weasel during a shoot walkabout, it is unlikely that you will see much of the animals themselves because stoats and weasels hunt most keenly during the last three or four hours of daylight and in the early hours of the morning.

If a dead rabbit is found and it is suspected that it has been killed by a stoat or weasel, it should be possible to check out your suspicions by looking at the neck of the victim. Sometimes a stoat will effect a kill by biting through the vertebrae of the neck, but it is more usual to find that the animal has thrown itself along the back of the rabbit and bitten through the jugular vein.

The best place to situate a trap will depend on the type of shooting and the topography of the land, but as a general rule thick undergrowth, brushwood, hollow trees, stone walls, hedge bottoms, ditches and drains make ideal trapping sites. It is not always necessary to make an elaborate

Any of the holes around the roots of this beech would provide an ideal site for a trap but in the top left there is a natural ready-made tunnel.

14

edifice; indeed, you will find that some of the most successful trapping areas result from the most natural-looking site which requires very little alteration in order to accommodate a trap. One point which you should always remember, if you are not to be forever catching the nose or paw of the dog, or trapping the odd pheasant or little owl, is the addition of two sticks pushed vertically into the ground at the entrance to the hole. The gap between them needs to be roughly 7.5cm–10cm (3–4in) and will prevent any accidental captures.

Where natural sites cannot be found, it is an easy matter to scoop out a narrow and shallow trench, place some boards or bricks over the top and cover them with soil. Both ends should be left open and the trap inserted from one end. If an artificial runway can also be included, it may help to funnel vermin towards the trap entrance. The positioning of these tunnels can be almost anywhere but some of the more successful places are likely to be along the top of a bank, by the side of a gateway or along the line of a barbed-wire fence.

At certain times of the year it may pay to use bait, especially when a 'dead-ended' tunnel is being used, or to use fresh urine from a dead female. Members of the old school of keepers say that blood will produce good results, especially on snow. Generally, though, it is not necessary to bait.

February and March are good times to trap because vermin have not begun to breed and there is not too much cover about. Remember to check that you have removed the safety-catch before leaving the site. Remember also that the trap must be positioned in the hole with the open jaws to left and right, not back and front.

Shooting

Much is made of the popular picture of the tweed-clad gamekeeper with his gundog by his side and a shot-gun under his arm, but in actual fact the gun does not play much of a part in the war against predators. To return to the Game Conservancy research, they found that amongst predators in general only 40 per cent were shot, whilst 60 per cent were trapped.

It may, however, be possible to shoot stoats, weasels and foxes by 'squeaking'. If you come across a fresh kill, it is worth the effort of standing quietly for a few minutes squeaking, either on the back of the hand, with a piece of grass, or with the aid of a specifically manufactured squeaker.

Crows and magpies are sometimes shot by the keeper on his rounds but normally they see a human being long before he sees them. It is slightly easier when they are nesting, especially when a hide is built near the nesting site. It has also been noticed that both magpies and jays are seized by a sort of nuptial fever as the weather becomes warmer, which makes them easier to stalk at the nest.

15

The popular image of a gamekeeper – unfortunately, the professional
has very little time to wander around with dog and gun.

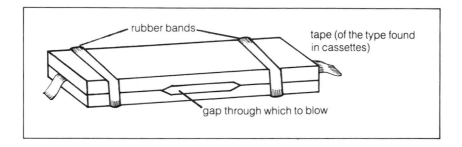

A commercially produced fox caller.

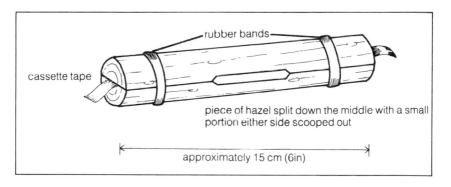

A fox caller which can be made at home.

Cage Traps

Cage traps are probably the best way to catch the avian predators, and the trap does not need to be an elaborate affair. Four old rearing sections tied together with a roof of wire netting works quite well. Funnels are made either in the roof or along the sides at ground level and a bait of maize, bread or carrion is placed inside. As the bird drops into the trap in search of food, the funnels will prevent it from walking out in the same manner as it entered.

Snares (Wires)

Unless you are prepared to spend many hours sitting in a tree, or downwind of a promising wood in the hope of seeing a fox, probably the only other practical method of controlling the fox population is the use of

17

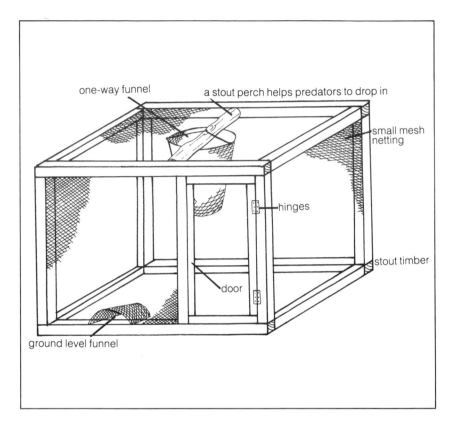

one-way funnel

a stout perch helps predators to drop in

small mesh netting

hinges

stout timber

door

ground level funnel

This cage trap could quite easily be made from redundant rearing field sections, or specifically made, as is the case here. Size is unimportant and pheasant catchers work equally well.

snares or wires. Fox snaring is not the activity most likely to endear you to the public but, provided that you use your best endeavours to ensure that no pet will be accidentally caught, snares are legal instruments and very effective.

Wires are best set in a gap in the hedge or along a narrow woodland ride. The gaps on each side can be bushed up with a few old branches and the wire set in the centre. Care must be taken that the ride or gap is not used regularly by either deer or badgers – it is better to place the wire elsewhere rather than risk catching either. However careful you are, the morning will come when something other than a fox is found in the snare. Normally you will be able to think of a way to release the animal

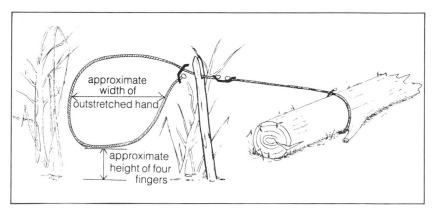

' There are as many different ways of setting a wire as there are people who set them.' This method works quite well, and if the snare is attached to a movable log rather than a static post or tree, the fox will drag it away a short distance and the snaring site can be used again.

unharmed, and to help you in your efforts it is not a bad idea to carry a pair of good wire-cutters in your pocket.

There are as many different ways of setting a snare as there are people who set them. Generally, one 'tealer' (a piece of hazel cut to about 30cm (12in) in length, pointed at one end and with a notch cut out of the other) is pushed into the ground and the wire is held up by being placed in the notch, so that the base of the noose hangs about a hand's height from the ground. The diameter of the noose again varies from person to person, but most keepers feel that the span of the outstretched hand is about right. Too open a wire and there is a danger that the fox may pass right through without being caught; too small and obviously its head will not fit through.

The Wildlife and Countryside Act

The Wildlife and Countryside Act of 1981 requires that both traps and snares are inspected at least once every 24 hours.

Rabbiting

Probably the farmer's greatest bugbear is having too many rabbits on his ground. How the problem is tackled depends on many factors.

The first consideration must be the time of year that rabbits are first seen to be increasing in numbers. Normally you would expect this to be during the summer, when the young rabbits are showing themselves and will be producing litters of their own. Late summer offers some of the best opportunities for shooting from a vehicle at night. Silage and haymaking will be over and some corn harvesting is under way. The ground will also be at its driest, giving the best chance for covering most of the farm whilst causing minimal damage to growing crops.

Because the fields are free of long grass, rabbits have to venture further from home in search of food. This means that it is possible to drive around the headlands and cut off their escape routes. Unfortunately, it also has the disadvantage of providing very little cover in which the rabbit can squat but a strong spotlight will help them 'freeze'.

Provided that a firearms certificate can be obtained, a .22 rifle is probably the best weapon, as it is quiet and so least likely to upset any neighbours. Ammunition is also cheaper, but obviously care must be taken when shooting on a place where footpaths and houses exist. You must, by

Entering the ferret. Stand clear of the hole and don't crash about!

law, get written permission from the landowner if you intend to use either rifles or shot-guns at night. It is also worth letting the local police know of your intentions as a matter of courtesy.

Ferreting

If it is found necessary to control rabbits in the winter, ferreting provides some good sport as well as being an effective method of control. If you use nets instead of shooting the rabbits as they bolt, there is no possible danger of disturbing the gamebird stocks.

The basic requirements are silence and stealthy movements (and, of course, a couple of ferrets!). The holes should be netted from the side rather than from above. Do not walk over the top of the burrow, and stand out of sight whilst waiting for the rabbits to bolt. It is not a bad idea to ban smoking, as a whiff of tobacco can cause a lot of unnecessary spadework.

Using small ferrets can help in avoiding hold-ups, as a small animal will find it more difficult to hang on to a rabbit than will a larger one.

Success! Put your foot across the hole or block it with a spade before dispatching the rabbit and resetting the nets.

Gassing

If all else fails, there is always gas on hand to help with eradicating the rabbit problem. The gas 'Cymag' seems to be becoming more difficult to obtain and is being replaced with a phosdrin-based solid sphere which is simply rolled down the hole. Even though it is easy to handle and a little safer for the operator, 'Phostoxin' should still be used with great care; you must read the instructions carefully before an attempt at gassing is made.

Final Points

Experience from keepering can help you to enjoy your shoot during the close season, as well as improving your prospects when the gun comes out again. As you go around your traps and wires, you will also increase your knowledge of wildlife. For example, by listening to the calls of jays in the woodland, you will be warned of the presence of rats, weasels, foxes, feral cats and even other humans. Blackbirds, too, are good indicators and to a trained ear there is a difference in each of these warnings, from a harsh, metallic sound to a noise like dripping water. The frequency also alters.

2
Location and Habitat

The whole point of taking on a small DIY shoot must be to give enjoyment to everyone who takes part. With no financial remuneration to consider, there can be no other reason, but it is not possible merely to blunder along. There must be some sort of organisation and an annual plan. These are often governed by the type of ground on which you find yourself. There is no point, for example, in taking on a solid lump of forestry and then getting excited by the prospect of releasing a pen of partridge.

With most of the country's best areas of rough shooting already taken and the popularity of such shooting forever increasing, you will probably have to grab at the first piece of land which becomes available and adapt your ideas to suit it, rather than the other way round, if you are to have any hope of achieving your ambition of running a small shoot.

Finding Somewhere to Shoot

Some people are very lucky and drop on to some excellent shooting ground without really trying. They may be good friends and neighbours of a farmer who decides that he wants something more than the odd Saturday afternoon walkabout, but has not got the time to waste rearing pheasant chicks. His neighbour may have both the time and interest to build a few pens, as well as being able to scrounge a few eggs from a nearby keeper and so, together, they have all the necessary requirements for a potentially good shoot.

Others are not so lucky and will have to make full use of the local grapevine in order to seek out any non-shooting farmers or landowners who may be prepared to rent them some ground.

Renting from the Forestry Commission

Occasionally, sporting tenancies are advertised in papers and magazines, but these are usually out of the financial reach of the ordinary game rearer. The Forestry Commission used to let out quite a lot of land at a reasonable rent but it has become noticeable that even its advertisements are

When attempting to rent a shoot, dark uninviting woods should be avoided like the plague, as the only attraction they hold is to a roosting pigeon on a windy, snowy night.

appearing with less regularity in highly populated areas, due to the conflict of shooting interests with the Commission's main objectives of allowing as much public access to its ground as possible. In less populated parts of the country, the Commission still puts some sporting rights out to tender. The whole acreage has to go as one block and there is no way that a small parcel will be let out to you separately from the rest.

Although putting the sporting rights out to tender, the Forestry Commission is not obliged to accept the highest bid and the area land agent will use his best endeavours to ensure that the person most likely to adhere to the conditions of the lease agreement gets the tenancy. All the conditions are laid out in the leasing document. A public liability insurance is transferred via the lease agreement. It states that the tenant has an obligation to keep down vermin and also states what you are allowed to shoot. This is not likely to include deer stalking, which is generally carried out by the Commission's own rangers.

The lease is non-transferrable except in certain cases, when an extra fee is required. There are legal reasons for the minimum leasing period being fixed at three years, but it is always possible to renew after this time, sometimes extending the agreement for up to 21 years. It is worth while knowing that not all land maintained by the Forestry Commission actually belongs to it, and that the sporting rights may have been retained by the proper owner.

Although planting policies and maintenance schedules are planned by the Commission years ahead, it should still be possible for a shoot representative to approach the area land agent and ask for permission to develop parts of its ground not currently being worked upon for the benefit of the shoot. Written permission must be obtained but it should then be possible to erect a release pen, or even dam a small natural stream in order to create a flight pond for ducks.

Obviously if the woodland on offer is dark, damp and unwelcoming, it is unsuitable for shooting and, unlike renting your shooting from a private landowner, there will be no opportunity to improve such a habitat. All is not necessarily lost, however – if the next-door farm is owned or rented but contains no space for a release pen, it may be possible to erect a release pen on the outskirts of the wood rented from the Forestry Commission, feed birds on to the farmland, preferably into a game cover, and then drive them back. It is unlikely that poults will wander through such dense woodland, preferring the more attractive farmland where they can pick about and sun themselves.

As far as the cost of rent per acre is concerned, it appears to be dependent upon the area and the suitability of the woodland on offer. As an aid to deciding a particular woodland's suitability, and whether it is worth letting sporting rights in the future, the Forestry Commission asks its tenants to fill in a Game Bag Return Form in which all that has been killed should be entered. It is in your own interests to do this, even though it could mean a slight increase in rent, because the Commission may consider nil returns to be an indication that the lease is not worth putting up for renewal.

Renting from Land Agents

It is often worth approaching the major firms of land agents, as they have offices in most parts of the country. Once again, the type of shooting likely to be advertised by them in some of the top sporting publications will be beyond the reach of most of us, but they do occasionally receive instructions to let smaller areas, of a few hundred acres rather than thousands, at prices which may be more acceptable to the small-scale game rearer.

Renting Dos and Don'ts

When leasing ground, from whatever source, do be sure to ask plenty of questions before signing a written agreement. If a map of the shoot is available from the landlord, walk around with him and clarify any doubtful points. Any rights of way should be pointed out, and any of the farmer's short-term plans outlined. For example, you may rent the sporting rights on the assumption that a useful looking wood in the bottom of the valley would provide a good releasing area in order to get birds into a block of kale at present planted on the horizon. It would then be disappointing to find that not only is the farmer winding down his dairy operations and will not be growing any more kale, but that he also intends to cut down the wood and flood the area to form an irrigation pond for his new potato-growing venture.

Some landowners will be only too pleased to let the shoot maintain their woodland. It is one less job for them and the layering of the outside hedge or the coppicing of a few acres of chestnut or hazel in order to create some ground cover will not only save money in maintenance fees but will also slightly increase the overall value of his estate. Others may resent and forbid any work of this nature, causing the shoot untold problems when it comes to planning a release pen site or when trying to thicken up a flushing point. I am sure that a compromise can be found between these two extreme cases, but it is as well to make certain before handing over any hard-earned cash.

There are obvious advantages in obtaining a long-term lease, preferably with an option to renew. There have been cases where friends have built up a reasonable shoot, only to have it taken away by a landlord who knows

The perfect set-up for pigeon shooting. The shooter is well camouflaged but able to shoot without hindrance.

a good thing when he sees it and realises that, now the work has been done, he and his own friends can benefit.

The Forestry Commission and established land agents have standard leasing contracts, but when dealing with an individual landlord it is advisable to get a written agreement drawn up by a solicitor. It may be decided that the best course of action is to take on the shooting for an agreed probationary period which gives both landowner and shooter the chance to part if things do not work out. Few landowners wish to witness a mob of armed cowboys wandering over their ground, leaving gates open, allowing dogs to chase livestock or shooting towards their neighbours' houses. The farmer who agrees to let out his sporting rights purely for the financial remuneration and has no interest in the actual shoot is not likely to prove a good landlord, and without his co-operation in keeping his dogs out of the wood, or not moving his cattle into the kale the day before a shoot, all is doomed to failure. Check too that he is not going to retain the right to shoot rabbits at night, as activity of this nature may disturb the pheasants.

The situation with farm staff will also need to be clarified. If they have been used to spending their Saturday afternoons pigeon and rabbit shooting, these activities will have to be dealt with by one means or another. The individuals involved either need to be stopped as part of the agreement, or included in the shoot, possibly undertaking midweek keepering duties in lieu of an annual subscription to the syndicate.

Improving the Habitat

Having arranged the lease and now possessing a satisfactory piece of land, much will depend on the limitations set out in the agreement as to how far you can go in an effort to improve the habitat.

Game Crops

The sympathetic farmer may be prepared to allow the shoot a few acres of his less productive ground in order to plant some kind of game cover. Admittedly, an unproductive headland along the side of a wood or thick hedgerow will not grow maize, millet or kale any better than it would a commercial crop of corn, but, as far as pheasants and partridge are concerned, it does not really matter. If nothing more than a few sticks of maize or kale grows, it will be sufficient to encourage a few gamebirds, especially during the early part of the season when temperatures are still quite high and the sun occasionally shines. Weeds will manage to establish themselves and their seeds are often enough to attract pheasants. It is not

Artichokes in their second year.

even necessary to plough and plant such a site in order to create a successful drive – the combine driver could merely be asked to leave a machine's width of growing corn along the headland. Provided his employer agrees, he will be only too pleased to do this and minimise the risk of damaging his combine with overhanging branches or fallen pieces of timber lying on the ground.

Mustard seed scattered into the stubble, or some of the sunnier parts of the hedge or wood, will germinate and will usually give sufficient cover for the early part of the season six weeks after planting, given the right growing conditions.

Artichokes are often mentioned as a game cover crop and they have the advantage of being perennial; once planted with a potato planter, they need no further looking after for several years. I have my doubts about the true value of this crop. It is said that pheasants find them attractive because they can scratch and peck at the tubers but, having worked on two estates where artichokes have been grown for the pheasants, I have never seen any evidence of this. However, they are definitely better than nothing, especially when planted along the side of a thick hedge in which a feed ride

Maize and millet mix: an ideal game cover, but one which will require a few tracks cut through it if it is to provide a sanctuary for gamebirds.

has been prepared, and shot before the frost has had a chance to knock the crop to the ground.

Maize, preferably combined with millet, is in my opinion the ultimate in game covers, and if a strip of kale is also included alongside it, the crop will produce a good drive throughout the season, provided that it is not situated in too exposed a place. There is often a problem in getting maize to grow, especially in the North, where the soil temperatures do not appear to rise sufficiently to ensure the seeds' germination.

Even when the farmer will not, or cannot, give over any ground to be used exclusively as game cover, he may still be prepared to plant crops required by him as feed in any case, in places beneficial to the shoot. Assuming that the farmer needs, say, five acres of kale as winter keep, it would be more difficult to flush game from it planted in one big block than it would if planted in a number of long, narrow strips. Strip grazing will sometimes effect this, but probably not until late in the season, when there is the added disadvantage of the continual disturbance caused by the herdsman daily moving the electric fence.

Hedgerows

It is unlikely that you will be consulted as to the removal of hedgerows if you are merely renting land, but the farmer's attitude towards them should become apparent during the early discussions regarding rental.

Generally, too many hedgerows are preferable to too few. They will always make a small drive and add a few birds to the season's bag. They could, however, have the effect of preventing birds from flying well, by acting as a screen for the guns. Whilst this is a good thing with partridges, pheasants need to be able to see guns as they fly from the cover if they are to provide an exciting, high shot. Taking out the tops of the hedges with a chain-saw will not only resolve the screening problem; the 'pruning' will also have a beneficial effect at the base of the hedge, encouraging new growth and strengthening up existing plants.

Woody and soft growth along ditches and hedgerows may also ruin a drive when birds are being driven towards them, as they often see such cover as a refuge and fly low with the intention of dropping into them. There is not always sufficient space to place the guns between the flushing cover and the hedge, but a couple of beaters waving flags will help if it is not possible to thin out the hedge or ditch.

If the farmer agrees to the planting of permanent game cover, he will probably also agree to the planting of a surrounding hedge which will act as a natural barrier to his livestock and give protection to the pheasants. The best methods of planting a hedge can be found in *The Hedging Handbook*, published by the British Trust for Conservation Volunteers.

31

Woodland Improvement

When taking on ground which has never been previously shot over, or has been neglected for several years, it is likely that the woodlands fall into two categories:

1. The overhead canopies of the mature trees may be so dense that light is unable to penetrate and the ground below is without any form of cover.
2. So much sunlight may have been admitted (especially when a stand of mature trees has been cropped and 'scrubby' timber such as birch and ash has regenerated itself) that it is impossible to walk through the resultant ground cover of bramble, and certainly impossible to flush a pheasant.

It is probably easier to create a good shoot from the latter than it is from the former. Cover is quicker to remove than it is to create. Good birds may be missed because of too much cover, so tracks should be cut through the bramble for the benefit of both beaters and pheasants. When it has been decided which way to drive a particular wood, the end at which the beaters start should be cleared of as much low cover as possible so that birds will be encouraged to run towards the flushing area. This in turn needs to be managed with great care if the shooting is not to be ruined by over-zealous clearing. A flushing ride is probably the first requirement and should be wide enough to run out a length of sewelling without it becoming caught up.

There should be a few cleared spaces immediately before this, so that the pheasants can make an unhindered take-off. In between these spaces, the thick cover must be left if you do not intend all the birds to flush at once. Ideally there should then be some medium-sized clumps of hazel or similar trees so that, once in the air, the birds are encouraged to continue rising until they fly over the mature trees at the end of the wood, presenting a good shot to the forward guns. According to the Game Conservancy, pheasants fly best when taking off at a 30-degree angle.

In woodland where no cover is to be found, some areas will need to be cleared in order to let in some light. Mature trees obviously cannot be removed without the prior permission of the landowner and, in some cases, a felling licence will also be required. The tops ('frith') can be left on the ground to help provide some temporary flushing cover, but beware of leaving too much, as too dense a clump will form a sanctuary for the pheasant but an impenetrable mess for the dogs and beaters.

Wider flushing rides will need to be cut so that birds can present themselves. If it is intended to stand guns in the wood, it may be necessary to cut out gun rides, or at least gun slots, so that a clear shot is possible. The most attractive coverts consist of scattered oak, birch and beech,

A wooden drum on a makeshift axle allows the playing out and
re-rolling of sewelling to be carried out with ease.

The flushing point, showing the ideal tree and scrub growth necessary to show a flying pheasant at its best – too steep and a bird will not be able to rise because of the struggle through tightly grouped trees.

with open glades encouraging a good growth of bracken and bramble. Holly, laurel and rhododendron bushes provide good shelter against rain, but it is better if they are allowed to grow tall – the taller they are, the more open they are underneath. If these bushes exist, there is no better situation for a feed ride or hopper. The birds have protection from wind, rain and overhead predators, and some interesting dry material in which to scratch. Incidentally, such habitat is also ideal for woodcock and if similar

Although 'skylighting' can only be beneficial to overgrown woodland, beware of leaving too much 'frith' which makes an impenetrable sanctuary for pheasants. On ground which harbours many deer, however, the protection thus given may be the only way of ensuring new shoot growth.

environments can be reproduced in other areas of woodland, it is often possible to encourage woodcock as well as pheasants. Any increase in the woodcock population will not be immediately apparent, however, and it may be five years or more before the results are seen in the season's bag.

Nesting Sites for Wild Duck

Mallard are stinking, dirty things to have to try and rear, so if the ground contains a suitable stretch of water it may not be a bad idea to encourage the wild population to do the work for you.

It is known that ducks have a 'home range' prior to, and during, the breeding season and it is the quality of the bird's habitat which decides this range. It must, therefore, be capable of supporting both adult and young.

35

A shallow, heavily plant-infested area is ideal for mallard (and snipe) due to the richness of insect life.

Suitable nesting sites are to be found in low ground cover near the water's edge but this will not necessarily be around the lake or pond, as a pair of mallard will more often than not make a nest in the bank of a small stream or ditch. Brambles, nettles, thistles and even ivy are favoured forms of cover and have the advantage of protecting the nest from predators.

Once the ducklings have hatched, they will be taken back to the pond. In order to increase their chances of survival, the water should be surrounded by gently sloping sides. If an island exists or can be created, it will break up any heavy waves which may otherwise account for quite a large proportion of duckling mortality.

A woodland pond suitable for flighting duck. However, the central island has too steep a bank for mallard to nest and ensure that their ducklings can scramble from the water without mishap.

Final Point

Before making a final decision on improving the habitat, whether it be for pheasant, duck or partridge, it may pay to consult the Game Conservancy's Advisory Department or, at the very least, ask the nearest approachable professional keeper for his opinion.

3
Rearing

Even when the amateur keeper takes on a shoot with the intention of relying on wild stock, it will not be long before he realises that a greater volume of sport could be had by rearing and releasing a few birds. So far it has been assumed that, because of limited time and finances, you are unlikely to be releasing any more than 500 poults. However, whether you intend to release five or 5,000, the principles remain the same, only the methods differ. Nowhere is this more obvious than when deciding upon a suitable method of incubation.

Although it seems that there is no point in the small-scale game rearer catching up laying hens in order to produce his own eggs, this does not mean that he cannot experiment with some kind of incubation. It is always possible to purchase sufficient eggs from a reputable game farm in order to fill a small 200-egg incubator. Otherwise, a bottle of whisky to the local gamekeeper will often be enough to ensure a couple of dozen pheasant eggs to set under a broody chicken!

Incubation

Bantams as Broodies

I have a preference for bantams over some of the larger breeds of fowl when it comes to setting eggs from either pheasants or partridges. However, provided that the breed is of the heavy, docile type, and will not habitually rocket through the door every time someone comes near the nest, there is no real reason why such a hen should not be used. Unless you have a very good friend locally, who is known to keep this stamp of poultry, and who will be prepared to lend one or two when they go broody, it will be necessary to establish a small chicken run in the back garden.

When a hen goes broody, she should be given a couple of days left alone in the chicken house. If, when you try to put a hand underneath her, she ruffles out her feathers, sits tighter into the nest and gives the back of your hand an almighty battering with her beak, you can consider her ready to set on some eggs, but not until then.

The eggs should have been obtained at the first signs of broodiness and left in an ordinary egg tray so that their contents can settle. It is a mistake to set eggs either under a broody or in an incubator if they have travelled any distance, as it is likely that the tiny 'shock absorbers' protecting the fertile germ in the yolk have not had time to return to their original state. Twenty-four hours is considered a sufficient period for this to happen.

A broody hen must have peace and quiet. Darkness or subdued lighting improves the steadiness of the hen. If a shed of some description is available, all that is required is a nest box of the right size, so that the broody can turn around and be comfortable without risking any of the eggs disappearing over the side of the nest and becoming chilled. For this reason it is not a bad idea to cut a grass turf, turn it upside-down and place it in the bottom of the box. Not only does this help to prevent eggs from rolling out when the rest of the nest is built up with hay, but it also helps to retain moisture and humidity, an important point when hatching any type of egg.

Probably the easiest way of dealing with a broody is using the

A broody bantam sitting on a clutch of pheasant eggs. Provided that she is warm and dry, no elaborate preparation is really necessary to ensure a good hatch.

old-fashioned coop and run. The coop will have a sliding shutter in the roof and bars along the front. Ideally, it should also have a shutter to prevent very small chicks escaping and predators, such as rats, entering. A wire-netting run can be made as long as conveniently possible and must fit flush with the front of the coop. It should also have some means of access. Make a shallow saucer-like depression in level ground and fill it with good, clean hay before setting the coop over the top. Fill any gaps with wood or bricks and then put in the eggs. Just how many will depend on the size of the broody but, as a guide, say nine for a bantam and 15 for a larger hen. There is a school of thought which says that an *odd* number should always be put under the broody, as this makes it easier for her to turn them. Whether this is true, I do not know, but it is interesting to note that any sitting of eggs found in the wild usually contains an odd number.

Broody hens should never be removed from the poultry house to the sitting box in daylight. The move must always be done at dusk, and the birds handled with great care.

If, after 24 hours, she is sitting tightly and happily, she should be encouraged to come out for a feed and drink. Once she is known to be well and truly settled it should be possible to leave the front open so that she can come and go to the feed as and when she pleases, saving you the trouble of lifting her on and off, risking smashing one or two of the eggs.

Once the eggs begin to hatch, the broody ought to be confined to the nest box and left well alone. As soon as the hatch has finished, try to move the coop and run on to some fresh, short grass. With the young chicks running about, it is even more important to ensure that the coop and run are on level ground and any holes, no matter how small, are blocked off, in order to prevent their escape. As the chicks grow, it is essential that they are given more room. If available, four rearing sections can be joined together and netted over, with the coop placed inside. Feather pecking is less likely with small numbers, but space is undoubtedly the determining factor.

Partridges and ducks are probably best reared by broodies, as it is unlikely that the small-scale rearer will wish to release any more than a few of either species in order to add a little variety to the shooting day. In this situation (provided the eggs can be obtained) either French or English partridges can be successfully reared by natural methods. English are notoriously difficult to rear by artificial means so, in the rest of this chapter, for partridge, read French. With the broody, however, there is no reason why a clutch of English chicks should not reach maturity.

Mallard can be reared quite easily, but they should not be allowed near any water in which they can cover themselves before they are almost fully feathered. An adult duck has oil on her feathers which becomes transferred on to the ducklings' 'down' as they creep underneath her for warmth.

Artificial Methods

Basically there are two types of incubator: cabinet machines and those which work on the 'still-air' principle.

Unlike a cabinet machine, where the air is moved around the interior with the aid of a fan or rotating paddles, in the 'still-air' model the heat is supplied to the top of the machine. Because there is such a variance of temperature between the top and bottom of the machine, it is vitally important to have the thermometer correctly situated above the egg tray, 6.4cm (2½in) above the egg, where the temperature should be 39 degrees Celsius (103 degrees Fahrenheit).

Professional hatcheries usually use a combination of the two systems. The eggs are first placed in cabinet machines, which are now so sophisticated that, once set up according to the manufacturer's instructions, they require very little human intervention. Turning is done automatically and the movement of a central rod up and down, in order to tilt the trays, is operated by means of a time clock and limit switch. The fan or paddles control the very necessary air circulation, whilst humidity is checked and measured with a contact hygrometer or, in the most up-to-date machines, electronic sensors.

Two or three days before the eggs are due to hatch, they are generally transferred to a still-air incubator or a specially designed hatcher where it is of vital importance that the correct humidity is obtained.

It can be seen that this large-scale incubating is a complicated business – for more advice on the subject, *see* Further Reading.

Cost and size will probably preclude the use of these large cabinet machines by the small-scale game rearer, but there are several 200-egg table machines with air circulation assisted by a fan which work on the same principle and should be more suitable.

Probably the most common types of incubator used by the amateur hatcher are still-air models known as the Glevum and the Ironclad. Originally they were heated by paraffin but over the years they have been converted to electricity by either the manufacturers or interested owners. It is however, sometimes possible to pick up a paraffin type at a farm sale, and there is no reason why it should not produce some very fine chicks.

Still-air machines being produced today (Vision, Curfew, Bristol, Marsh Roll-X, etc.) all work on basically the same system and, whilst electricity is used instead of paraffin, are all variations on a theme.

With the Glevum and the Ironclad, heat is passed to the top of the incubator and the temperature is regulated by means of a damper. This is raised or lowered by the expansion and contraction of an ether-filled capsule situated on a cradle near the top of the eggs. Humidity is supplied with the aid of two sliding water trays, which must be kept filled at all

A large automatic incubator, made under the name of Western.

times, and at the base of the machine is an arrangement of two or three felts. These are removed one by one at intervals of a week and let out stale air.

Immediately below the egg tray is a flat tray on to which a piece of hessian is usually tacked. A glass panel fitted into the door immediately at the front of the egg tray encourages the chicks, as they hatch and dry off, to make their way towards the light. They then fall through a gap and on to this hessian tray. When the hatch is complete, they can be removed to the brooder house.

During the whole of the incubation period, the eggs in these small incubators need to be turned twice daily by hand, in order to prevent the developing embryo from sticking to the side of the shell. In a natural situation, it has been calculated that a broody hen turns her eggs once every thirty minutes or so, and I believe that the large incubators, in which eggs are turned automatically, are programmed to turn every hour. One way of ensuring that each egg has been turned is to mark them with a cross on one side and a nought on the other. By making sure that all crosses are showing in the morning , and noughts at night, twice-daily turning seems to be sufficient to produce good chicks.

It is also important that the incubator is housed in a suitable shed or building which retains a constant temperature. A brick building with good insulation is likely to produce better results than a draughty wooden shed or, worse still, a tin one, where the temperature fluctuates dramatically every time the sun shines. The ideal temperature is probably around 16–21 degrees Celsius (60–70 degrees Fahrenheit). Adequate ventilation is important as the machines take in fresh air and give back stale. If the room feels at all stuffy it could be affecting the egg. A concrete floor is a good idea – not only is it easier to keep clean and disinfect, but also, as hatching time approaches, it can be kept damp so as to improve humidity in the incubator.

Buying in Chicks

There are several advantages in buying day-old chicks from a game farm or other reputable source. First of all, it cuts down on some initial capital outlay, namely that of purchasing and maintaining an incubator and filling it with eggs. Secondly, if a large shoot with a full-time keeper decides to buy in at day-old rather than hatch its own, the decision will probably have been made to give the keeper more time to concentrate on his predator control and woodland management. The same applies to the part-timer who could use any spare time to encourage his wild bird stocks. Thirdly, if the shoot owns two brooder houses, each capable of rearing 250 birds, then 500 chicks can be ordered, a delivery date guaranteed and the season's rearing programme completed in just six weeks.

Rearing

Siting the Rearing Field

There are many methods of rearing pheasants and partridge. If the rearer has access to some large buildings, it may be a simple matter to section off one end of an unused shed in order to house an infra-red heater, gas brooder or electric hen and make a small portion of grass or concrete accessible by means of a pop-hole knocked through the wall.

If it is intended to rear by Calor gas (probably the most common method in use today) a suitable rearing site needs to be found and properly maintained. Even if you are rearing a few birds for your own shoot in the privacy of your back garden, you need to have a piece set aside from the family flower garden if your activities are not to disturb the status quo!

A suitable rearing field needs to be well drained – look for it in the winter months when the ground is obviously at its wettest, bearing in mind that thunderstorms can cause flash flooding when the ground is baked hard and surface water is unable to penetrate. It should also be properly fenced if there is any danger that neighbouring farm animals could break in and smash the equipment, or even merely rub against the sides of the shed and inadvertently cause the premature release of the pheasants.

Although it may at first seem a good idea to position the brooder houses under trees in order to protect them from the hot summer sun, in practice the temperatures inside the sheds are harder to maintain. This does, however, have the effect of keeping the interior darker and thus cuts down on feather pecking, but birds will not do as well and, on balance, if trees have to be included in the site, position the large outdoor runs under them, leaving the sheds and night shelters in the open.

The grass on which the birds are going to run should not be left so long that a white fungus can be seen when you push a hand towards the roots. This encourages a disease called *Aspergillosis* which can seriously affect gamebird chicks. Some keepers like to see a good growth of grass, believing that it cuts down on feather pecking, but it must be remembered that young pheasants can become disorientated under such heavy cover. At the very least, therefore, cut tracks around the perimeter of the outside runs and also in the shape of a cross through the middle of the area where the outside runs are to be sited. This will help the chicks to find their way back to the heat. If they cannot, they will crowd in the corners and either

Good fencing around the proposed rearing field is essential if you are
to prevent accidental access by farm stock.

be missed when shutting up or become chilled. Because of this, many
keepers (and I am one of them) prefer to mow all the grass on the rearing
field, but the argument of long versus short can only really be decided by
individual experience.

Finally, eradicate all signs of moles on the rearing field, not because they
are potential predators on the chicks but because it is not uncommon for
weasels to use mole runs to get under wire and pen sections.

Building a Rearing Unit

You only have to take a glance at a game farming catalogue to see that it is
an easy matter to buy all the necessary game rearing equipment. However,
even the cheapest price quoted is likely to be far greater than the cost of
building your own shed, night shelter and sections.

A brooder shed 2.4m×1.2m (8ft×4ft) is large enough to rear 250
pheasant chicks successfully. Increase the width to 1.8m (6ft) and it is
possible to rear 300-plus birds. The latter will require a larger, slightly

Three outside runs, 9.1m×9.1m (30ft×30ft) *in situ*: the nets are kept out of the keeper's way by means of poles, with plant pots to prevent the poles from wearing holes in the netting. The straw bales provide a distraction for growing poults.

more expensive heater, but just how much bigger depends to some extent on the height of the shed – the more air space there is, the greater the heat needed to fill it.

The dimensions of the shed are 2.4m×1.2m (8ft×4ft) with the height from floor to roof being 1.2m (4ft) at the front, dropping to 0.9m (3ft) at the back. A door should be situated in the middle of the front panel so that there is easy access to feeders and drinkers. Small windows are fitted at either side of the door. Actually, 'windows' is rather a grand title, as you do not need glass, just small-mesh wire over which a sliding shutter arrangement is made. It is important to have enough ventilation and, to be sure of this, extra holes can be drilled along the top of the front section in order to expel used and stale air. These must, however, be fitted with baffle boards. Pop-holes are fitted at either end of the shed so that the night shelter can be attached at the most convenient point.

It would be logical to make the night shelter the same size as the shed, and the roof section must be covered over. Some manufacturers and

Brooder house front. A central door provides easy access and
windows need only be mesh, covered by an adjustable shutter. Baffle
boards at the extreme top protect ventilation holes.

keepers clad the sides and ends with some form of perspex or plastic;
others just run a nylon sheet over a netting frame from the front of the
roof to the bottom of the back section, leaving the front and ends exposed.
Personally, I think this arrangement is best, allowing the birds some
protection, but at the same time hardening them off more than they would
be in a totally enclosed area. When this method is being used, it is
advisable to drive a couple of posts down beside the two front corners of
the night shelter which in turn are either wired or nailed to each post. On
an exposed rearing field the wind may otherwise get under the nylon sheet
and carry the whole edifice several metres away.

The brooder shed is made from plywood and 5cm×2.5cm (2in×1in)
battening. The sections for the night shelter are made from the same size
battening, as are the 3m×1.5m (10ft×5ft) sections used when constructing the large outside run. All sections should include a softwood bottom
panel about 46cm (18in) high in order to protect the young chicks from
cold winds.

Rearing Procedures: Day-Old to Six Weeks

It is important that, when the day-old chicks are first placed in the brooder house, they learn the source of heat as soon as possible. When rearing is being carried out in a large shed, this is best achieved by making a circular surround of cardboard or hardboard. Not only are the birds guided towards the heat in this fashion, but they are unable to find a corner in which to crowd, suffocate, chill, or do any of the other things which pheasant chicks seem to take a delight in.

The heat source is suspended from the ceiling at a height which ensures that the temperature on the floor directly underneath is about 32 degrees Celsius (90 degrees Fahrenheit). Each week its height from the floor is progressively increased until, by the third week the temperature is down to about 21 degrees Celsius (70 degrees Fahrenheit). Many Calor gas heaters include a control knob on the regulator and, if this is the case, you can use this to turn down the heat rather than having to fiddle about with

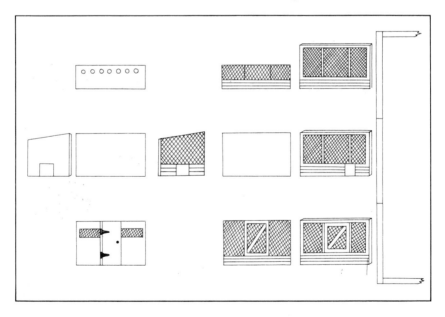

Laying out the rearing unit. On the left is situated the brooder shed, attached to which is the night shelter, either totally enclosed by Monoflex weatherproofing material, or with roof and back protected by means of waterproof sheeting. The large outdoor run is made up of twelve sections: ten plain, one pop-hole and one gated. An overhead net prevents escapees.

adjustments inside the shed. After a few days, the cardboard surround can be moved away completely, but when part of a large shed is being used, it will pay to increase the size of the surround gradually until the young poults begin flying over the top (at about ten days). Then it can be moved and the birds given the opportunity to use all the available floor area. It is vitally important that a chick is never allowed to get chilled. Although placing a cold bird back under the heat seems to revive it, a very high proportion of these casualties develop gastro-intestinal problems or liver and kidney failure and will probably die a few days later.

It is nearly as important not to let the chicks get too hot and much can be learned by watching them closely for the first couple of days – they are, after all, the best guide to the correct temperature. If they are seen to be huddled under the heater, they are undoubtedly too cold. There should be a centre spot which is too hot, with a ring of comfortable chicks around it. If you watch an individual bird from this ring, you will notice that every so often it will get up, have a run around, try out the food and water and then return for a quick warm-up. If the circle of birds is found right against the cardboard, then the chicks are too hot and the cardboard ring should either be enlarged or the heating arrangement raised.

A cardboard surround will prevent chicks from crowding in the corners.

Most keepers use wood shavings as a covering for the floor and also to bank up any corners in which the chicks might congregate. These will almost always be flattened the next time you take a look, but it is always worth banking them up again or, better still, cutting triangular pieces of plywood which can be slipped into the corners and used year after year. When using electric hen brooders, a piece of hessian should be positioned immediately underneath the unit. This has been found to prevent chicks from scraping a hole in the shavings and then being suffocated by the others lying on top of them. Do not, however, use any smooth material for this job as it will cause some of the chicks to become splay-legged.

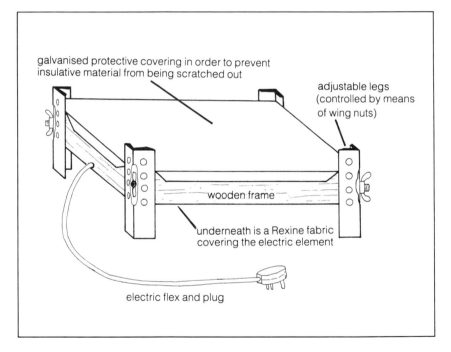

The electric hen brooder, probably only of any real use to the game rearer who intends to rear poults in part of a large building where the electricity supply is already incorporated. Provided the building itself is reasonably warm, and heat from the brooder is not being taken up in order to warm the atmosphere rather than warm the chicks, good poults should result. Remember to include hessian or corrugated card immediately underneath the heater. This will prevent losses as chicks scratch into the wood shavings and others climb on top, causing unnecessary deaths from suffocation.

Feeding and drinking vessels are the next requirement and should be placed around the heating area (not in it), so that the chicks do not have far to go to look for food. Small jam-jar type drinkers are ideal for the first two or three days but, small as they are, it is still possible for a chick to drown, so it is not a bad idea to place small pebbles around the base of the drinker. Alternatively, and probably easier when changing the water twice daily, a small piece of piping can be used. By placing the drinker on a piece of scrap hardboard, the water level is maintained and the shavings are less likely to get wet. For the first three days I like to include an antibiotic in the water.

Food is usually given for the first few days on egg trays (*see* Chapter 5).

Depending on the weather conditions, it should be possible to let the chicks into the night shelter during the first week. For obvious reasons, the grass must be tightly clipped. Again depending on the weather, chicks can be let into the main outdoor run at about two weeks old. They are still very small at this stage, so you must be doubly certain that any holes or gaps are filled in, preferably with stones or bricks. If chicks of differing ages are being reared next to each other, and the pen sections are used as a dividing wall between the runs, any of the younger group which do manage to scramble through to the others will undoubtedly be killed.

Feather Pecking

When even a few pheasants are being reared artificially, feather pecking is sure to surface. It is thought to be brought about by boredom or stress. Young individuals are picked on by the others who will keep at the bird until it is merely a dead and almost unrecognisable mess. Then they will start on another, and it can lead to big losses if nothing is done.

Chicks reared under an infra-red lamp tend to start pecking earlier than usual, maybe as early as two days old. This probably happens because they are in full view of each other. In this case it is preferable to debeak the chicks quickly and simply by using an ordinary pair of nail clippers.

Poults of differing breeds and colours should, where possible, be reared separately. This is especially important with melanistic or white chicks, as the white wing feathers create an immediate attraction; once blood is drawn from the tips of the wings, this in itself forms a focal point on which the others can concentrate.

At three weeks, irrespective of whether there has been any outbreak of pecking, you will need some form of protection against its occurrence. There are special debeaking tools on the market which operate from a car battery and slice neatly through the upper mandible whilst at the same time cauterising the cut, thus preventing bleeding.

Debeaking must be pretty stressful to the poults, but then so is bitting if carried out in a rough and careless manner. However, the fact that many more game rearers prefer to bit rather than to debeak must tell its own story, and I personally feel that bitting is the lesser of two evils. The bits can be made of either plastic or metal and they are inserted between the upper and lower mandible, being held in place by the bird's nostrils. Although plastic bits may work loose, they are, in most people's opinion, preferable to metal ones. When the birds are released, the plastic variety can be removed with a twist of the fingers, whilst the tougher metal bits need to be removed with pliers, causing even more stress. When ordering bits, ask for 'B' size.

Final Points

Give yourself plenty of time to prepare for the rearing season and keep a stock of spare parts such as nozzles, air filters and fuses. Have gas heaters checked over annually by a professional Calor gas supplier and do not be tempted to overcrowd the sheds.

Remember that not all birds will reach the age of six weeks and do not get too despondent if a few chicks die. Even experienced keepers consider

Plastic bits prevent feather pecking. The three-week-old bird on the left is fitted with size 'B'; the week-old on the right with size 'A'. (As a gauge of size, they are held in the hands of a seven-year-old boy.)

A distraction as simple as silver foil will often help to prevent small quantities of poults from becoming bored and more vulnerable to feather pecking.

themselves fortunate if they lose only 10 per cent of their initial stocks, and they often lose a lot more. Treat any advice you are given, or read, merely as a guide. So much depends on weather conditions and individual circumstances. If you are told to turn off the heat at three weeks and do so religiously, crowding may occur on a chilly night after even the hottest of summer days.

4
Releasing Techniques

By virtue of their size, and the fact that no amateur keeper can spend as much time on the ground as his professional counterpart, small shoots are rather prone to the allegation that the birds which they shoot are not always their own. The best way to keep on good terms with your neighbours, especially when they rear and release a large number of poults, is to release some birds, even if only a token amount. It is not always possible to find the time or finance to carry out a rearing programme on even the small scale described in Chapter 3, but the shoot can still release a few birds by buying in poults from a local game farm.

Pheasants in a small laying pen. At the end of the laying season, birds may be offered as shooting stock, but whether they are a viable proposition is open to question.

It may not be only time or finance which prohibits the shoot from rearing its own birds. You could have problems in obtaining a rearing field on a rented shoot if no member of the syndicate has adequate ground on which to position a couple of rearing sheds. For such shoots there are two alternatives: buy in either adult ex-laying birds or six-week-old poults.

Not many keepers feel that ex-laying birds are a worthwhile investment as, even though they are wing-clipped and treated in exactly the same way as poults, they do seem to have a habit of disappearing at the first opportunity. Most people prefer to buy poults; the prices are comparable and the returns are likely to be greater.

With either system there is the added advantage that you pay for what you release, unlike rearing day-olds when, to release 500, it is necessary to purchase perhaps 750 in order to allow for losses. A disadvantage of buying poults (and it is only a minor one) is that if the game farm has agreed to deliver on a certain date, it is unlikely that they will be able to postpone that delivery if the weather is wet or cold, and some losses may occur as a result.

Releasing Broody-reared Poults

In the days when all pheasants were reared by the broody method, all the chicks were kept in the coop with the broody hen on release day, a horse-drawn trailer was borrowed from the farm and, at daybreak, coops, hens and poults were loaded up and transported to a suitable site prepared in the woods.

Some small-scale rearers still use similar methods and perhaps put coop, hen and poults inside a small pen built from four rearing sections netted over. After a few days, one or two poults are allowed to walk out through the gate; at night they will return to the pen to be near 'mum' and the other chicks. As the keeper feeds and waters them each day, he then lets another couple out until all the birds are released. The broody can then be taken home again, or let out to encourage the poults to roost.

Special care must be taken that foxes do not find the birds during the first couple of nights, when it is likely that they will still be 'jugging' on the ground outside the pen and form an easy meal. It may be worth while to obtain a roll of the Flexi-net type of electric sheep netting and a cheap fencing unit, which would offer some form of protection and take very little erection. Other deterrents include flashing roadside lamps, feed sacks hanging from the trees, creosote or diesel spread around the area, or, possibly, a radio left on all night.

Flexi-net in use. Although it is being used in this situation as tree protection against rabbits, a roll of this material will offer protection against foxes when small pens of pheasants are being released.

Releasing Partridges

Partridge pens can be protected from the unwanted attention of predators by similar means as for poults and, of course, one or two fox wires in the immediate vicinity will help if the chosen site for the pen is alongside a hedge or in a narrow ride. Apart from wires, it may be possible to call up a troublesome fox by squeaking. Patience will often be rewarded if the approximate area from which it comes is known. A high vantage point is the best way of obtaining a shot and a comfortable tree should not be difficult to find if you have done your homework. If there is no convenient natural high seat, then position yourself downwind of where the fox is

An easily constructed high seat. Although the most common use for a seat of this nature is in deer stalking, when it is important not to let the quarry catch sight of you nor scent you, one or two seats on the shoot provide ideal points from which to shoot a fox or merely watch the poults return from their day's wanderings.

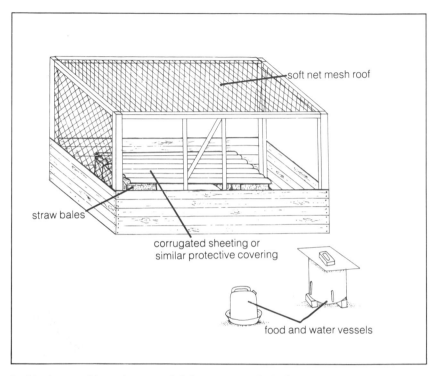

soft net mesh roof

straw bales

corrugated sheeting or
similar protective covering

food and water vessels

Inside the partridge release pen it is important to include some
protection from the weather as well as food and water. Although not
shown here, there should also be a similar shelter on the outside in
readiness for when the birds are released.

most likely to appear. Correct calling is also important, and two or three
squeaks should be followed by periods of silence.

No matter whether English or French partridges are being released, or
whether they have been reared by bantams, artificially or bought almost
fully grown from a game farm, the accepted method of release is similar to
that used for releasing broody-reared pheasants. Four pen sections with a
netted roof covering are erected, inside which should be placed a couple of
straw bales with a piece of corrugated tin or scrap board laid over the top
as a protection against bad weather. A hopper of the kind from which they
will be expected to feed once released should also be included, as must a
drinking vessel.

For both English and French, an identical arrangement should be made
on the outside of the pen whilst French will also appreciate a bale of straw

placed tight against the pen itself so that they can stand on it and keep in touch with those birds still to be released. The bale seems not to be so important for the English partridge, who keep in contact with each other verbally rather than visually. An experienced partridge keeper of my acquaintance claims that English will not use a bale as a vantage point, and that he has won many a bet by spotting partridges some distance away and persuading his companion to guess what variety they may be. His method of telling was: if they're on a bale they must be French, if not, English.

Like broody-reared pheasants, partridges are leaked from the pen a few at a time but at least a pair should be left in the pen throughout the season in order to encourage the remainder to return to the area. If, however, this couple escapes, the returns do not seem to be greatly affected.

There appears to be an optimum time for holding partridges in the pen. Generally, 25 are put into each pen about a month before shooting commences and are held for about two weeks before the first few are released.

The siting of the pen is important and some of the best results are

Preparing for partridges in an ideal situation. Although full of weed, the maize will nevertheless keep birds around the pen, and the dairy grazing on the horizon gives them an alternative.

obtained if it is erected at the flushing end of a game crop. One which contains maize and kale and is surrounded by arable and dairy grassland cannot fail, but the rough shooter will probably have to compromise and experiment for a couple of seasons in order to find the best spot. Towards the end of the shooting season it is not uncommon for French partridges to leave the fields in favour of the woodland and they often become regular feeders along the pheasant rides. Because of this, French have occasionally been released with the pheasants in the release pens. Such an operation is, however, doomed to failure and it is better to take the time and trouble to release them by the more orthodox methods.

Woodland Release Pens

All shoots, whether releasing 100 or 10,000 poults, must have some form of pen in which the young pheasants can become acclimatised to the wild after their six or seven-week stay on the rearing field. The most popular system used to liberate poults is the large open-topped pen.

Siting

The basic idea behind the positioning of the release pen is to choose an area where birds can be fed away and then driven homewards. In some situations they can, however, be used to attract pheasants from the main pens into an area which would otherwise be unproductive. This 'decoy' pen only needs to be small with just a few poults released into it, but the fact that pheasants are there compels the keeper to feed daily. His whistling, and the natural noise and activity caused by the birds, will often encourage the majority of pheasants to use the site.

There is a danger in having too many pens and, contrary to what you might expect, too many may even cause a reduction in the number of birds shot during the season, due to the lack of time available for correct maintenance. It is probably better to have one central pen containing 500 poults, than five pens of 100. It is only possible to feed one pen at a time, and if you have four or five, you may have to begin feeding before all the birds have come down from roost. Remember that when the time comes to feed all the out-tracks, it will take twice as long to get around and unforeseen problems such as a branch falling over the pen wire will obviously require prompt attention.

The first essential is to identify the most suitable site for your release pen. Ideally the site should be as close to the centre of the shoot as possible and should contain a certain amount of bramble, hazel and mature trees. Although some ground cover is essential as a protection against the weather and overhead predators such as sparrow-hawks, too much may cause poults to become lost upon release. Therefore, if you need to take in a tractor and swipe in order to erect the perimeter wire, it is not a bad idea to cut out a few rides within the pen area itself at the same time.

It is also important to include a few sunning areas so that the poults have ample opportunity to dry out after a shower of rain, or merely to indulge in a dust bath and a spot of sunbathing. If the gate is built to correspond with one of these sunspots, it will be found that the tricky problem of getting birds to feed immediately after their release will be that much easier.

Although it is tempting to include a stream within the pen, to do away with the daily time-consuming and boring job of filling water troughs, its inclusion could cause problems when treating the inevitable outbreak of disease. Access to natural water needs to be prevented in order to be sure that poults are only drinking prepared water into which medications have been carefully measured.

If a stream or ditch is included, there could be another, more serious disadvantage. Mink are becoming more widespread and their numbers are not necessarily confined to large areas of water. Indeed, at certain times of the year, they seem to prefer small tributaries or streams and if the one which they choose leads to a pen of vulnerable, newly-released poults, they need go no further until they have either killed all the birds, or have themselves been caught by the keeper. Like the fox, mink do not content themselves with one kill to provide a meal and will continue killing for the fun of it. Unlike the fox, they can squeeze through the anti-fox grid in the side of the perimeter wire and are not too afraid of a human presence.

Construction

Once a site for the pen has been chosen, its size and construction must be considered. The pen should be big enough to allow plenty of room for each individual pheasant, cutting down the risk of outbreaks of feather and vent pecking. Build the pen with a view to the future and make sure that it is large enough to include more birds next season when, flushed with the success of this year, you will undoubtedly wish to release even more and further upgrade the shoot. Avoid making it too large, however, as this increases the risk of poults getting lost. The Game Conservancy recommends approximately 1m (3ft 3in) of perimeter netting per bird, although this ratio may be almost halved for numbers of between 500 and 1,000 poults. The actual height of the wire netting varies between 2m and 3m (6ft 6in and 9ft 10in) and is usually made up of two rolls: 3.2cm (1¼in) for the lower half and 5cm (2in) for the upper half. The bottom 23cm (9in) is turned out and pegged down or buried, whilst the top 46cm

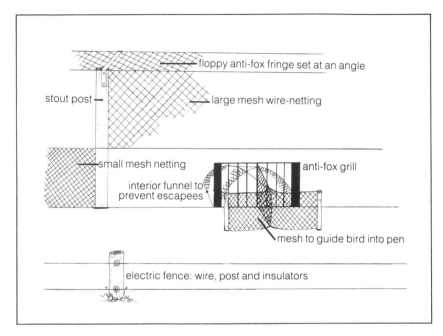

floppy anti-fox fringe set at an angle

stout post

large mesh wire-netting

small mesh netting

anti-fox grill

interior funnel to
prevent escapees

mesh to guide bird into pen

electric fence: wire, post and insulators

A section of a pen complete with all possible predator deterrents.
Every effort should be made to create the best possible release pen and
prevent entry by predators. Although a single roll of wire netting
wrapped around a few trees will contain the newly released poults, it is
not likely to stop foxes or feral cats.

(18in) is allowed to flop outwards in order to prevent foxes or feral cats
gaining access. Most keepers see the value of further protecting their pen
by adding an electric fence 23cm (9in) out from the base of the pen and
23cm (9in) above ground level, with a second strand being placed 23cm
(9in) above the first.

Some years ago, Game Conservancy researchers developed an anti-fox
grid which is now seen in the perimeter wire of most release pens. The idea
of this grid is to allow poults re-entry to the pen once they begin to fly over
the wire netting. It must be fitted with 'wings' which lead out from the
entrance and help to direct the pheasants inwards. On the inside of the
grid is fixed an inverted wire-netting funnel so that birds wandering up
and down the inside of the pen cannot simply walk out.

If time permits, you may be able to include a few little extras when
constructing your release pen. Dusting shelters, for example, will be
appreciated and much used by the poults and they are easy to construct.

A dusting shelter within a release pen. Not only does it offer
amusement for the newly released poults, but on wet days it provides
a dry spot in which to feed.

Four posts are set out in a square, the two at the back being about 50cm
(20in) above the ground, the two forward ones being about 1m (3ft 3in)
above the ground. Across these are laid spars long enough to support
about three sheets of corrugated iron which form the roof. It is preferable
if the shelter faces south, as it then becomes a sun trap and is protected
from the worst of the wind. As the soil dries out, the young poults will use
it to dust and very shortly the area will contain only fine particles. A
quicker method is to dump any fine ashes left over when cleaning out an
open fire.

Preparing for Release

Although it pays to shut in the poults on the rearing field for as long as
possible, at least a week before they are due to be released they should be
allowed to spend nights outside in the open runs. Naturally, they should
only be allowed to do this if the weather is likely to be fine. During a heavy

Until the age of about four weeks, poults should be pushed into the brooder house at night to prevent any possibility of chilling in the early hours.

thunderstorm, instead of finding a dry spot in the night shelter or brooder shed, they will either crowd into a tight bunch or congregate in the corners and, even at this late stage, losses will result. They do need some form of hardening off before being taken into the release pen, and a cool night with an early morning dew definitely helps to create a hardier bird.

You will have to find time to clear any overgrown vegetation in and around the release pen. Even a new pen constructed earlier in the year should be checked once again for holes in the wire or escape routes where rabbits may have tunnelled in and out. The electric fence line should be sprayed with some form of weedkiller such as Gramoxone. This will prevent the regrowth for at least six weeks of any vegetation which may cause the fence to short-circuit.

If the pen has been *in situ* for a season or more and the wire has been lifted to allow the beaters access, before pegging it down again, it would be wise to run a dog through the pen to make sure that a fox has not taken up residence in the ground cover. I know of at least one occasion where this simple operation was neglected. The result was that nearly all the poults

Spraying around the electric fence with Gramoxone. Note the height at which the two wires are fixed to prevent access by foxes or wandering dogs.

released were killed on the first night by a litter of part-grown cubs which had been trapped inside the pen! Traps and fox wires should be placed around the pen and in the immediate vicinity.

If you propose to hopper feed, these should be filled before releasing the poults. If you are hand feeding, a good covering of pellets along the ride will help the birds to settle in. Make sure that there are plenty of water vessels in the pen – five-litre chemical drums (well washed out, of course) cut in half, polythene sheeting sunk into shallow depressions dug into the ground, and dustbin lids or car tyres cut in half all provide adequate drinkers. Place them along the intended feed ride so that the poults will find food and water all together.

There is some argument amongst keepers as to whether straw should be used along the feed rides in the release pen. Some feel that it encourages fungal diseases as it builds up from year to year, whilst others like to include it as it keeps the poults occupied by giving them some good

Taking poults to wood. Beware of overcrowding the crates on a warm day. For crates of this size, 34 birds per crate is generally the right number, although in the early morning, with only a short distance from rearing field to release pen, the numbers could be increased to as many as 50.

scratching material. It also soaks up the wet and mud during a rainy spell and encourages the birds to associate straw with food – a useful fact when birds begin to look for feed rides in the woods outside. If you decide to make use of straw in the release pen, wait until the pheasants are used to the feed ride and pecking about for their food before including it.

Moving Poults to the Pen

With large numbers of birds to take to the release pens, I always make an early start on the morning of a releasing day. In fact, if the weather is settled, I catch up the first batch of poults the night before, placing them 34 birds to a crate. At first light (about 4.30 a.m.) I have them loaded up

When clipping or pulling the wing of a six-week-old poult prior to release, remember to remove only the first ten primary feathers on one wing.

and into the release pen. With the second batch I put 50 birds into each crate as it is cool enough for them not to 'sweat up'. After breakfast, I cut down to 34 per crate again, as by that time the day is beginning to warm up. By following this procedure I can have 1,000 poults released by lunch-time, giving them the rest of the day to get used to their new surroundings. Because allowing birds to get used to their surroundings is an important factor in successfully releasing them, never continue a releasing programme after about 3 p.m.

On the selected day, remove the plastic bits and pull or clip the flight feathers of one wing as you place each bird into the carrying crates. It is better to do this on the rearing field rather than in the release pen, as one or two birds are bound to escape as you grope about in the crate trying to catch hold of them. Most crates are fitted with a sliding door as well as one in the top, so if the pheasants are clipped on the rearing field they can be allowed to make their own way out of the crate and will therefore be less likely to suffer from stress.

Only the primary flight feathers are clipped or pulled. There are ten of these, but if poults are released after the age of six weeks, some new, adult feathers will be growing which, once cut, will not grow again until the following year. If you have had to keep poults back longer than normal, because of poor weather conditions or for some other reason, pulling the wing feathers is a better idea than clipping, as nature will replace pulled ones but not cut ones. The idea behind wing clipping is that the poults will not be able to start flying out over the release pen wire for three or four weeks, by which time they should be accustomed to feed times and their new environment.

Care after Release

Eventually the poults will be flying off the roost over the wire and landing perhaps a field away from the release wood. For a day or two they will be so shocked by their own bravado that they will rush back to the security of home as soon as they land. If the keeper is there to whistle them back and to feed them (*see* Chapter 5), this will help them to form an association with the pen and its surrounding woodland.

At both the early morning and evening feed, every opportunity should be taken to walk around the outer pen perimeter and push escapees back into the pen through the anti-fox grids and funnels.

Pheasant poults returning home via the anti-fox grill.

Protection from Predators

It is about the beginning to middle of August that foxes may become a greater problem than usual and kill poults as they land outside the pen. One way of telling whether a dead bird is a fox casualty is the fact that all but the head, legs and wings will have been gnawed clean. Another indicator is several birds found uneaten, or poorly buried under leaves or soft earth. Cats will bury their kill but usually make a better job of it than the fox.

There may also be predator problems within the pen itself. Tawny owls can be quite a nuisance and one way of checking whether they are the culprits is to look for marks along the neck or back. Occasionally the back of the head has also been smashed in.

A sparrow-hawk does its damage during daylight hours and can take birds away to feed its young ones, leaving no sign of anything being wrong. You should always be on the look-out for signs that your poults do not wish to feed. It may not be because they are not hungry, but because they are afraid to venture out from cover when a hawk is hunting in the area. If you are quite happily hand feeding and the pheasants are responding well until a pigeon, or even a blackbird, flies over and causes the whole lot to scatter, you can be pretty sure that there is a sparrow-hawk troubling them. If a sparrow-hawk's kill is found, the breast area is generally eaten first. There are no legal ways of eradicating birds of prey but it is possible that owls may be deterred by flashing lights or by hanging feed sacks about, and sparrow-hawks by strips of silver foil strung across the pen on cotton.

When the poults begin to wander off and take no notice of the feed whistle, the hedges and areas which the pheasants seem to favour can be 'dogged' back in the pen direction, if you have the time and a suitable dog. Although the poults need to be given space to explore, total freedom may result in them wandering off on to a neighbour's ground, never to return. If that neighbour is also a shooting man, there is an unspoken rule about not dogging-in along that boundary, as one shoot is bound to benefit from the other's birds.

If you can find the time to dog-in on the way to work and on the way home, take full advantage of the fact that when pheasants wander they travel on foot, but fly when pushed homewards. This operation may increase their flying capabilities and will certainly make them more wary of people and dogs on the shooting day.

Stubble Burning

Birds leaving the pen may start to jug in newly-cut cornfields rather than return to the security of the pen. Dogs prove useful in preventing this dangerous practice. In being sent homewards the poults are protected from predators and from stubble burning, when it is carried out at the end of a day's combining.

Generally speaking, stubble burning is a bad thing as far as shooting is concerned. Poults could get burnt; there is the danger of accidentally setting fire to important hedges and shelter belts; and there is a longer term effect in that burning destroys vital sources of insect food and low cover.

Releasing Problems

By the end of September you will have noticed that there are more birds feeding on the outside of the pen than inside. When this happens, some keepers lift the wire and give their pheasants total freedom, yet allowing them to return to the usual roosting trees. The outer electric fence should help to deter foxes and the poults by this time will be fully winged and able to roost well out of danger. Feathers which have been damaged by the unwanted attentions of the others are also given the chance to regrow.

Flushing birds homewards. As birds begin to wander from the release
pen, the keeper should spend some time in persuading the newly
released pheasants back to the pen. Your dog's breeding and
obedience are of secondary importance and here both spaniel and
terrier are being used.

Lifting the wire does, however, have the disadvantage of releasing birds
left in the pen, the only ones over which the keeper has any control. Even
when given the opportunity of returning under the fence, many poults
prefer to stand under a group of bushes and wait for the keeper to throw a
handful of food which they may or may not deign to accept!

You will notice that individual birds, identifiable by certain characteris-
tics and markings, have moved away from the pens and you can assume
that others will have followed. In an ideal world they would have waited
until you fed them away into the surrounding woodlands, from where
they will eventually fly and provide a good sporting target. However, you
will probably have to chase after them with straw bales and a feed bucket,
in a desperate attempt to persuade them to stay wherever they can be
found. Admittedly, there is not much else which can be done at this late
stage, if the improvements have not been made earlier in the year and if
rearing and releasing techniques have not been correctly carried out. Apart
from perhaps cutting and nailing branches along the top of forestry rabbit
netting, to aid the comings and goings of the pheasants, you just have to
cross your fingers and hope for the best in the coming season.

Combined deer and rabbit netting of this nature often renders a wood
useless for pheasants. Access and exit are almost impossible but
perhaps some branches nailed across the posts could help.

Undoubtedly birds will disappear, and it is impossible not to worry but, unless they are totally neglected, there will still be some there for the shooting day.

Releasing Mallard

Mallard are usually released at around six weeks of age. They are very often reared and released as an afterthought and as a result give a disappointing return.

Obviously they need careful attention if they are to fly well, and one of the basic mistakes that many keepers make is to overfeed. A small release pond is not necessarily a good idea, as the ducks get very little exercise and thus have no inclination to fly. Feeding is all important (*see* page 86), but neglect seems to be the order of the day. In a previous job I used to release a few mallard. I tended to rely on their lazy nature and never clipped their wings. Feeding was carried out as and when I remembered, but the end results would have been the envy of many top pheasant shoots! (Perhaps I was just very lucky.)

It is best to section off a portion of the chosen pond with wire netting or, if the water is very shallow, use some discarded pen sections. Some land should be included but, because ducks can take to the water if danger appears, the height of the wire is not as important as it is for pheasants. Feeding continues in the shallow areas and, in an effort to encourage birds to fly, some keepers feed their ducks away from the water, at a vantage point from which they will fly well. But if it is not felt necessary to clip the wings, why put birds at risk from predators?

The shooting of reared duck gives rise to some ridicule in the sporting world. There is one shoot at least which makes no secret of the fact that all the ducks shot on a let day have been walked into a cattle wagon, taken to the highest point and then almost thrown out by hand in order to create a decent shot. In an effort to prevent such diabolical methods, it behoves the small-scale rearer to create a better environment in which birds will fly well and naturally.

Final Points

No matter what is being released artificially, the largest mortality rate is likely to occur between the ages of six to twelve weeks, so it is important to do your best at this time. However, feeding is an important factor and correct management at this stage will make the world of difference in the months to come.

5

Feeding from Day-old to Sixteen Weeks

One of the most mundane of the keeper's duties is that of daily supplying food and water to the poults. After the age of six weeks, incorrect feeding, either by giving too much or too little, may result in pheasants wandering off the estate, whilst bad management from day-old will produce either weak and underdeveloped birds or dead ones. Correct feeding is therefore nothing less than an essential part (perhaps the most essential part) of the successful day-to-day running of any shoot and should be carried out as

Chicks pecking at a finger ring, showing the interest they have in anything shiny: a useful point to remember when trying to encourage day-olds to feed.

74

meticulously and with as much punctuality as you can manage.

There is a danger in rushing out and buying new, innovative products, guaranteed to make life easier; it is interesting to look back through shooting magazines of ten years ago and see the various advertisements claiming to ' . . . stimulate feeding and introduce essential nutrients at the earliest stage in the bird's life . . . the revolutionary new food additive . . . ' You may wonder why, if they were so good, they are not forming a vital part in today's feeding programmes.

A few years ago 'holding blocks' were formulated, claimed to be the ultimate safeguard in dissuading poults from wandering and especially valuable to the part-time keeper. Undoubtedly pheasants do like them and peck away quite happily, but a small heap of grain-store sweepings, occasionally replenished and perhaps topped off with a part-bale of straw, will have the same effect.

Day-old to Three Weeks

The sooner you can get the newly hatched chicks interested in food, the better chance they have of surviving. Chicks hatched or adopted by a broody hen cause the operator very few problems, as the hen will pick up the crumbs provided and drop them in front of her charges, encouraging them to eat with a few clucking noises. With only a small shed of artificially reared chicks and plenty of time at your disposal, it may be possible to emulate the hen's methods by tapping with your fingers on the feed tray. They will be attracted towards such activity, especially if you happen to be wearing a finger ring.

The fact that chicks are attracted towards anything bright can be used to advantage when encouraging the first attempts at feeding. A sheet of tin foil covering the bottom of the feed tray has a dual effect: firstly, the chicks peck at any pieces of foil showing between the particles of crumbs and by accident begin to pick up the feed, and secondly, as the birds run across the tray, the tin foil causes the food to spring up and down and they peck at it out of curiosity.

Other methods of encouraging gamebirds to pick up food include the addition of chopped hard-boiled eggs. I am told the following works quite well but it cannot be said to be conducive to hygiene: if live maggots are dropped into the feed, the chicks are supposed to be attracted by their movement and, like the foil idea, will pick up crumbs by accident while attempting to capture the maggots.

For the first few days access to the food should be made as easy as possible and probably the best feeding vessel is a large egg tray. They are cheap, hygienic and disposable. The moulding stops the chicks from

An egg tray makes the ideal food container for the first few days.

scratching too much food over the floor but at the same time allows them to get right in amongst the food. There is bound to be some wastage but in my opinion this is preferable to losing chicks through starvation. The egg tray must be pushed into the wood shavings to prevent any chicks squeezing underneath and getting trapped. After the first week, normal chick feeders can be used, but remember, when using those designed for the poultry industry, that broiler chicks are larger than game birds of the same age, so make sure that the lip or rim is not too high off the ground.

From the age of day-old to three weeks, chicks should be fed with properly formulated pheasant starter crumbs. If you are also rearing partridges, either with a batch of pheasants or separately, then 'super' starter crumbs should be used for the first week. Although these are identical in make-up to the ordinary crumbs and contain the same protein, they are much smaller and give a better chance of survival. Many keepers who deal only with pheasants prefer to use 'super' starter crumbs for the first week before going on to the ordinary crumbs.

Water is best given in old-fashioned and cheap jam-jar drinkers, but remember to put either small stones or a piece of hose around the bottom for a couple of days (*see* page 51).

It is possible to buy a vitamin supplement which is added to the water for the first three days of the chick's life, but I personally would advise the use of Terramycin, a very safe antibiotic, unlike *some* vitamin preparations which, if incorrectly mixed, may well poison birds. Terramycin is also useful at other stages of the rearing programme. If used two days before and after bitting is carried out, and also two or three days before taking poults to wood, it helps to cut down the losses from stress.

There is a time (about five days after hatching) known by keepers and game farmers as *starve out day*. You expect to pick at least one dead bird each morning of the first week, but on starve out day the numbers will peak and the newcomer to game rearing, if not forewarned, will undoubtedly panic, thinking that his chicks have succumbed to some major disease. The reason for these deaths is, as the name implies, that weaker chicks have not learned how to feed and drink and have by that time used any reserves absorbed from the egg sac.

Adequate feeding and drinking points aid in a fast start to feeding, as well as helping to prevent overcrowding in any one point, thereby reducing the risk of feather pecking. Do not, however, place the feeders and drinkers so close together that water is carried into the food, causing it to become sour and stale.

Three to Six Weeks

Although three weeks is the time usually given by most feed manufacturers as the date to change from crumbs to pellets, from my experience it pays to start introducing pellets a little before that. There seem to be two reasons. Firstly, I have noticed that chicks are looking for something else in their food after the age of about two weeks. Scientifically, I could not justify that statement. However, from several years spent observing the activities of pheasants in my charge, there is a certain point where, although the food seems to be disappearing, if you look closer, the crumbs which you fondly hope are disappearing down the pheasants' crops are in fact being scratched into the floor covering. Secondly, it is unfair to change the feeding policy at precisely three weeks when, if you follow the earlier advice on bitting and debeaking, the two operations coincide. How can a bird be expected to cope with a strange object which is suddenly stuffed in between its nose and beak, as well as a change of appearance in its dietary requirements?

Make sure that the next stage of food has been ordered well in advance and begin to introduce pellets *very gradually*, perhaps one part pellets to three parts crumbs.

At this stage the birds should also be well used to feeding from hoppers or chick feeders in the night shelter, as well as finding and using drinkers both there and in the outside runs.

There are two types of pellets used on the rearing field: mini pellets replace starter crumbs, whilst growers' pellets replace the mini variety at some point between the ages of four to five weeks. Apart from the possible problem of expense, there is no need to rush birds from one type of pellets to another. Provided that the manufacturer's recommended sequence is followed and that the food has been prepared specifically for the needs of gamebirds, not ordinary fowl, protein requirements necessary at various stages of the poults' growth will be guaranteed, plus protection from the

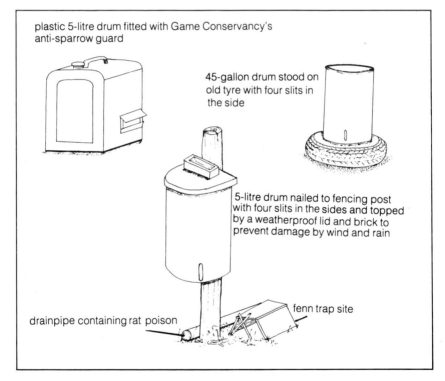

plastic 5-litre drum fitted with Game Conservancy's anti-sparrow guard

45-gallon drum stood on old tyre with four slits in the side

5-litre drum nailed to fencing post with four slits in the sides and topped by a weatherproof lid and brick to prevent damage by wind and rain

fenn trap site

drainpipe containing rat poison

Three types of home-constructed hoppers. Although only the central hopper is shown with points for rat poison and a tunnel trap, any site where it is intended to supply food on a regular basis should be equipped with some means of preventing wastage by vermin. It is, however, essential to prevent access or the accidental capture of any other forms of wildlife.

worst of diseases in the form of added antibiotics or preventive medications.

The type of pellet you happen to be on at the time of releasing poults is the one which should be offered to the birds in the release pen. They have enough problems to contend with, without changing their diet, and the transition to covert or poult pellets should be made as and when the young pheasants are fully accustomed to their new environment.

Before the birds leave the rearing field, however, every effort should have been made to ensure that this transition is less harsh by adopting the feeding system that you plan to use in the release pen. If you intend to use hoppers, hoppers of the same type should be used in the outdoor runs for at least the final week. When sufficient time is available to allow for hand feeding, then (if weather permits) begin throwing pellets on the ground in both the run and the night shelter.

If hand feeding is decided upon, some means of attracting birds to the rides is needed and most keepers simply whistle. This is probably only because you can never forget your mouth, and apart from on a cold morning, when trying to whistle at seven o'clock is practically an impossibility, whistling is a good idea. Banging a feed bucket or bin with a

The author whistle-feeding his newly released poults.

In dry weather, piles of food left in the rearing pen will accustom the poults to being fed on the ground once in the release pen.

stick, a dog whistle, or even a vehicle's engine regularly used near the feed ride, will have the same result. Pheasants must be accustomed to the feed whistle or attracting noise by the release stage, or very soon afterwards. So, even before taking birds from the rearing field, withdraw surplus food and replace ad lib feeding with regular hand feeding. The secret of a successful season is to maintain the interest of poults without keeping them hungry or too well fed. If starved after release, they will wander in search of food in the same way that a poult too well fed will wander because of boredom. Start this procedure on the rearing field. Birds will, when first faced with a whistle, disappear towards the safety of the night shelter or brooder house, but if their education is continued, it will only be a matter of days before poults associate the whistle or similar noise with the fact that food will be available very shortly.

Hopper Feeding

Almost any container which is waterproof and vermin-proof can make a suitable hopper for pheasants or partridges. It is possible to buy specifically built self-feeders which are in use in the poultry industry, or even fully automated ones designed with the particular needs of gamebirds in mind. These automatic feeders are very expensive but, provided they are kept full, they will, by means of a hooter, call the birds to the area and distribute the amount of food the feeder has been programmed to deliver at any time you wish.

There is no need to go to all this trouble, however. Five-litre drums (metal) can, in a very short space of time, be fitted with four slits, either in the sides or underneath, stood on a couple of bricks, filled with food and be fully operational. The Game Conservancy have taken the idea one stage further and it is possible to purchase guards from them which allow gamebirds access to the food, but not sparrows or squirrels.

Some keepers prefer to use 50-litre drums stood on an old tyre or two straw bales, or to attach the five-litre version to a fencing stake. Others get more technical altogether and devise a pendulum system whereby food is released to the floor when the pheasant pecks at a swinging plate under the hopper. This is traditionally known as the 'Cumberland'. The 'Whitlaw' hopper varies from the others in that it is made in the way that most children draw the cradle used by Jesus immediately after his birth. Obviously it is fitted with a waterproof lid and the underneath is covered with small-mesh wire netting through which corn is encouraged to trickle when the birds peck.

Not only does a hopper look better painted green or brown and will last longer for being thus protected, but it will also be less obvious to the

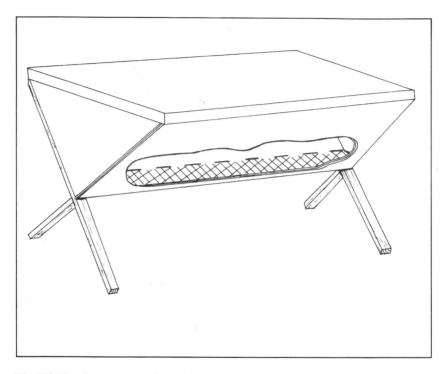

The Whitlaw hopper, complete with weatherproof lid. The dotted lines indicate the wire mesh grille through which the corn falls when pecked at by the pheasants. Straw added to the mixture prevents the wheat from falling out too rapidly. Alternatively, include several layers of mesh in order to make the apertures smaller.

casual passer-by. Another good idea is the inclusion of a tunnel trap in the vicinity of the hopper and also rat poison placed in drainpipes.

Six to Sixteen Weeks

Assuming that poults are feeding well on the release pen rides, wheat can be introduced into their diet round about the age of twelve weeks. Some rather short-sighted employers, in an effort to cut down on costs, insist that their keeper starts feeding wheat as soon as birds go into the release pen. This is far too soon, as there is not enough goodness in a grain crop for a bird to both survive and grow. The introduction of wheat should, like the different stages of pellets, be brought about very gradually. Maize,

Grit left in appropriate piles around the food and water supplies will
help the birds settle to their new surroundings.

either whole or split, can be used shortly afterwards, but use it sparingly as
it encourages birds to put on fat and may, in extreme cases, kill them or at
least prevent them from flying well.

I have noticed that after a certain time pheasants become bored with the
covert pellet which will have been brought into their diet at some time
between the ages of six and eight weeks, so it is unnecessarily expensive to
continue feeding pellets when you notice that birds rush along the feed
ride picking up wheat and maize in preference to the pellets.

Ordinary poultry grit should have been made available to the birds right
the way through their life, but now that natural foods and grain are being
picked up in and around the release pen, its provision is doubly important,
as it is used in the gizzard for grinding up food passed there from the crop.

Attracting Birds to Outside Woods

Once a few birds have been seen flying out of the pen and drifting down certain hedgerows, you will need to begin feeding in places other than the release pen in order to control them and draw them towards woods or game covers. If hoppers are to be used, ideally they should first be placed outside the pen and then progressively moved closer to the outside wood or game cover, say one move every other day, until birds are happily travelling between the pen and the new feeding area. Hand feeding is carried out in the same way, increasing the distance between feed area and pen. Devoting the amount of time necessary to encouraging birds across may be impractical, so rides will just have to be made in the woods or game crops and food left there in the hope that the poults will eventually find it. More often than not they do, but do not be discouraged if there is nothing to be seen for the first week. Take great care not to throw too much feed along the ride when hand feeding these new areas or you may end up with a better grain crop than the farm!

When cutting a feed ride in either wood or game crop, try to start at a point nearest the release pen. The cut area should never reach all the way to the edge of the cover because an open-ended ride will let in the wind and give the birds a feeling of insecurity. In game crops, it will also pay to make several other tracks through the crop, cutting across the direction of the proposed drive. As beaters push through the cover, any birds running ahead of the line may take to the wing as they break into the open cross-tracks, rather than running on to the end of the drive. These tracks should be about 3m (9ft 10in) wide – any less and birds will tend to run across the gap.

Make the feed rides in the woods as long as practicable in order to give the birds the best possible chance of finding them, and also to prevent any bullying. Ideally, the ride should be cut at an angle, or curved, in order to prevent the wind and prying eyes. A good proportion of ground cover at either side of the ride is also a necessary requirement so that the birds can hide in it and feel protected should they be disturbed.

Most shoots include straw on the feed rides and may also lay a line of bales along a sunny hedge with feed on top of them. There is no doubt that pheasants enjoy being that little bit taller, obtaining a better view of their surroundings. Of course, the straw on the feed ride is spread about a little and not left in a bale, but there is no need to be too precise in its distribution as the birds will scratch about for food and in a very short time will have made a good job of levelling it. Because of its colour and 'scratchability', the inclusion of straw definitely helps to attract poults and also prevents a certain amount of theft from sparrows. In exceptionally wet weather, however, straw may be less preferable than leaves or peat which

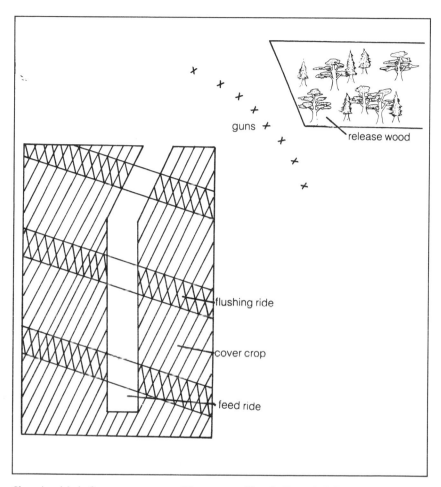

guns

release wood

flushing ride

cover crop

feed ride

Showing birds from a cover crop. Pheasants will only fly at their best
when being pushed homewards, preferably over a valley in which
guns can be positioned. Cutting flushing rides at various points
through the crop will encourage birds to flush throughout the drive
rather than running forward and flying *en masse* upon reaching the
end of the drive.

dry out more quickly. If holly or laurels can be included as part of the feed
ride, such leaves and friable soil are easily found by the pheasants.

Whilst taking out straw bales, a few feed bins should also be taken to the
feed ride and filled. This will save a lot of foot-slogging with sacks when it

is impossible to get a vehicle across because the stubbles have been ploughed or the ground is too wet. The first filling will probably include some covert pellets so only fill them with as much food as will be used up before the time when you expect to be feeding grain only.

Feeding Ducks

Ducks feed at night and rest by day, so if yours disappear at night and return in the early morning it can be assumed that they are using your pond as a resting area and you will need to shoot in the early mornings. If, however, you are lucky enough to possess a feeding pond, the ducks visiting it need to find sufficient food to make them want to come back. As the number of ducks increase, more food must be put down, but beware of giving them too much, as instead of rushing in at dusk they may prefer to turn up as and when they feel like it, maybe even as late as midnight. In extreme cases, they may not even leave the pond and will certainly not provide a sporting shot.

A pile of barley left for ducks will encourage an all-year attendance on the flight pond and will ensure the arrival of a few young birds.

In an ideal world you would put down exactly the right amount of food a few minutes before the birds arrive. Barley, wheat, split maize and rotten potatoes are all a good meal for mallard. Begin feeding in the early part of August and, as a rough guide, remember that a two-litre bucket holds about 5.5kg (12lb) of corn which will be enough to feed about 75 ducks.

Final Points

If you are lucky enough to have a crop such as maize planted near the release pen or, in fact, anywhere on the shoot, it must be borne in mind that such natural food will take the edge off a pheasant's appetite and, as a result, birds will not necessarily be present in such large numbers as they would otherwise be around the woods and release pens. An abundance of natural food such as acorns and beechmast will, like the positioning of maize or similar game crops, have an obvious effect on the whereabouts of birds.

Feeding on the truly wild bird shoot where no game is reared must begin before autumn and ploughing commence.

Finally, many keepers swear by the use of certain oils in order to keep pheasants at home. By all means try them. However, from experiments carried out under the supervision of an interested local chemist who suggested several ways in which to conduct trials, and supplied the mixtures of oils most commonly used by the more old-fashioned keepers, the conclusion was reached that if birds did become attracted to these mystical mixtures over a period of time, it was only through an association of ideas, in that the smell was connected with the arrival of food. Regular whistle feeding would no doubt produce just as successful a result.

Whilst beating on several shoots, I have noted pieces of rag hanging on the feed rides, protected by old sheets of tin, and smelling of aniseed. Perhaps the pheasants are supposed to become 'high' on the oils and, presumably, are unable to travel from the shoot in their stupefied state – possibly a new meaning for the phrase 'high flier'?

6

Common Diseases

When rearing game birds artificially and intensively, it is not always possible to prevent disease. Some of the more notorious diseases which troubled keepers of a decade ago are now no more than minor ailments, due to the fact that many proprietary foods milled specifically for gamebirds contain coccidiostats and antibiotics which are added by the compounder at a preventive level. This does not mean that the disease will not occur, only that it is less likely to do so. In some ways, the addition of medicines by the food manufacturer could be said to a disadvantage to the keeper, as they often mask some of the first signs of an outbreak of disease, so you must keep a careful look-out for anything unusual. Like the farmer leaning over a five-bar gate watching his stock grazing, you should make time to watch your birds both on the rearing field and in the release pen. A word of warning: if this period of watching happens to be after poults have just been fed in the release pen, do not automatically assume that they have gapes when you notice them standing with necks outstretched and gasping for air. It is more likely in this case that, like many youngsters, they have bolted their food rather more quickly than is good for them!

Take care too when adding drugs to the food at a curative rather than preventive level, and be aware of the fact that an overdose in gamebirds is just as dangerous as in humans.

Hygiene

It should go without saying that hygiene is an important factor in producing a healthy pheasant but, although we all start a new rearing season with the best intentions, it is not long before any antiseptic footbaths, provided to prevent the accidental spreading of disease by visitors to the rearing field, become filled with rainwater, and the concentration is never remixed. Dead chicks which were at first meticulously removed and buried or burnt remain lying on top of the brooder shed until they disappear in a rotten, maggoty mess or are taken by the local magpies.

If it has been necessary to cut grass in the night shelter or outdoor runs, do not leave it in a pile thinking that it will provide amusement for the

Disinfecting the brooder sheds prior to erection.

chicks. It is more likely to become mouldy and infect the birds with one of many fungal diseases.

Clean and disinfect rearing equipment, both when putting it away and when re-erecting it in readiness for the coming season. The disinfectant should be one specifically produced for the poultry industry and preferably one which is 'Ministry Approved'. If the farm on which the shoot is run owns a high-pressure hose, this is a useful piece of equipment.

Many people feel that a good coating of creosote not only protects the sheds from the elements, but is also useful in controlling the spread of bacteria. *Never* creosote a shed or building a few days before you intend to use it for rearing, as the fumes are poisonous to most forms of livestock. The operation is best carried out in the autumn when putting sheds, sections and the like under cover.

Naturally, the longer you rear or release on a certain piece of ground, the greater the chance of disease. Certain manufacturers claim that their products will kill microbes and parasites on open ground, but it is the opinion of most veterinary authorities that there is no known cheap and practical means of killing all infective bacteria. Where possible, then, the rearing field should be moved every few years, and if there has been a particularly high level of disease, the Game Conservancy recommends that 'the land should be ploughed, heavily limed and cropped. It should in any case be allowed to lie fallow for at least one full year.'

Some Common Ailments

Coccidiosis

Coccidiosis is the most common disease on the rearing field and normally affects chicks of between three and five weeks old, although it has been noticed in some as early as ten days old. There are no definite symptoms but the affected bird soon becomes noticeable by its dejected appearance, ruffled feathers and occasionally blood-stained droppings (although this is more commonly found in the type which affects poultry). The droppings, whether blood-flecked or not, will probably be white, sticky and copious. A lack of interest in food is another indicator.

There are three forms of this disease, the most common being that which affects the bird's caecum. Usually all three are present, but the main give-away is a mass of cheese-like substance in the 'blind gut', apparent when the carcass is opened up. The disease is caused by a microscopic parasite which ruptures the blood vessels in the intestines; this, in turn, infects millions of cell vessels and the cheesy material is in fact a mass of these cells which have died.

Mixing Amprol-Plus to cure Coccidiosis. Always add the solution to the water rather than water to the solution if you wish to avoid a bubble-bath effect!

Red-legged partridges are affected by a different parasite and display different symptoms, often dying quickly and unexpectedly without any loss of condition.

The most common cure for coccidiosis is Amprol-Plus solution, which is given in the water and will effect a cure without any danger of toxicity from overdosage, caused by the addition of a coccidiostat already present in the food. To find out exactly what is in the food, look at the label, which will be marked ACS as well as giving the name of the coccidiostat. Amprol is given for at least five days, depending upon the severity of the outbreak.

Coccidiosis is species specific, that is, although a turkey and a pheasant may have access to the same ground, it is impossible for the turkey to infect the pheasant and vice versa. Obviously the turkey could infect another turkey, and the pheasant another of its kind.

Blackhead

Blackhead, once more common in gamebirds than it is today, affects both the intestine and the liver. Deaths often occurred in poults of good condition, although sometimes a yellow diarrhoea was noticed, together with a loss of weight and an inabilty to do more than wander around in a drunken stupor. Nowadays, if these symptoms are noticed, they are likely to indicate a disease relatively new to gamebirds: hexamitiasis.

Hexamitiasis

This disease has been noticed by keepers predominantly when birds are in the release pen, although the Game Conservancy points out that birds of a few days old can be affected and that the disease is likely to cause the highest death rates at about two weeks of age.

Trichomoniasis

Trichomoniasis has been found to cause similar symptoms to hexamitiasis, and both diseases are treated with the same drugs. They are both caused by microscopic animal parasites which live in the gut. Whilst they may occur together in the same bird, research shows that trichomoniasis is most common in the partridge.

I have many keepering colleagues who, along with myself, have had birds with one or both of the diseases, but it has only occurred with poults in the release pen. Possibly the most noticeable sign that all is not well is that, although there is a tremendous increase in the amount of food consumed, this is not being used in the development of the bird and, over a period of time, the poults become extremely thin, losing virtually all their breast muscle.

Emtryl soluble powder is the preferred drug for the treatment of either hexamitiasis or trichomoniasis, and in extreme cases it may need to be used alongside Terramycin.

Gapes

Everyone interested in shooting and keepering has heard of gapes and the gapeworm, so much so that you often get the impression that this parasitic worm is a friendly little chap. Keepers talking amongst themselves tend to say, 'Oh yes, I've had gapes again this year,' almost as if they have the gapeworms in for a drink!

The disease has been around for a long time and before there was any treatment, keepers would try all sorts of methods to rid themselves of

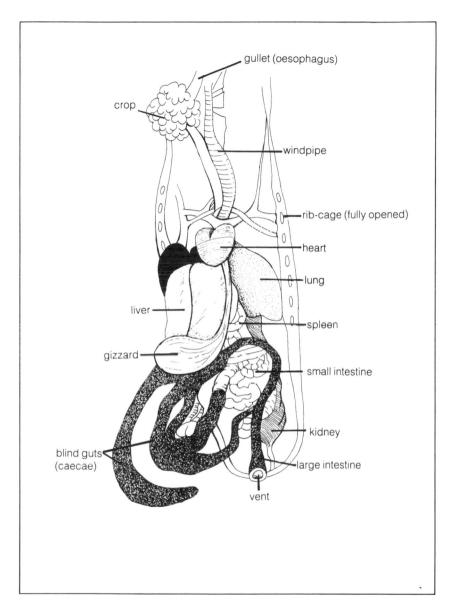

Even a rudimentary knowledge of the internal workings of a gamebird will prove useful when the amateur keeper finds a dead bird on the feed ride.

gapes. One trick was to strip down a feather until only a few strands were left at the very tip. This was then dipped in liquid paraffin and pushed down the bird's beak, hoping to reach the windpipe and dislodge the worm. Things are a little more scientific these days but, although gapes has been recognised for a long time, it is still capable of causing the death of young poults if left untreated.

Pheasant poults suffering from gapes will 'snick', perfectly described by the Conservancy as being ' . . . an action which may be described as a cough accompanied by a sideways flick of the head.' Partridges, instead of coughing, may merely appear to be gasping for air, with their beaks open wide.

Mebenvet can be added to the food by the pellet manufacturer and will successfully cure poults within about ten days. When dealing with small numbers of birds, however, it may be necessary to buy Mebenvet in sachets and mix it into the food yourself, as it is unlikely that the compounder will mix up an order for only a few bags.

Gapex is added to the water and is claimed to cure birds within 24 hours. Wormex is a liquid added to the food and is supposed to have the same effect. I have found a reluctance on the part of the poults to pick up pellets which have been thus treated, but several friends swear by it and use it in preference to Mebenvet.

Final Points

Most adult birds carry a certain number of internal parasites but, as a rule, these cause no harm. The same cannot be said of poults, and confined birds, either on the rearing field or in the release pens, are subject to constant reinfection from their own droppings. In such cases, the parasitic burden can build up very quickly and very dangerously.

It is, therefore, absolute folly to let any suspicions that birds do not appear as they should go unattended, in the hope that they are merely off colour and will be 'all right in the morning'. Swift action is preferable to hoping that sick birds will recover, and any delays may result in more deaths.

The Game Conservancy is the only body of people to specialise in the welfare of gamebirds in general, and to research into gamebird diseases in particular. Although many vets have a certain amount of knowledge regarding poultry, they cannot be expected to diagnose the specific diseases of pheasants and partridges, so the only available alternative for the game rearer who suspects problems is to make use of the post-mortem service offered by the Game Conservancy. The cost is immaterial as there is no way that it will exceed the overall cost of the pheasants which would otherwise die. If you live close enough to deliver birds in person, so much the better; the solution to the problem will be available by four o'clock the same day. If not, send diseased specimens by first-class post, well packed and preferably nowhere near a weekend when post will be delayed. Mark the parcel 'Laboratory Specimens – Urgent'.

This chapter has only dealt with the more obvious problems likely to occur on the rearing field and in the release pens but, as long as you are prepared to admit defeat and ask for further assistance when coming up against some of the less common diseases, all is not necessarily lost. In any case, it will pay to buy the Game Conservancy's green booklet no. 6, *Diseases of Gamebirds and Wildfowl*.

In an effort to combat certain diseases, the shoot should order some medications in advance. Terramycin, Amprol-Plus and Mebenvet will cover the most common diseases, but Emtryl could also be bought and stored. It is better to be ready for any eventuality rather than waste time in procuring certain medications once a disease has been diagnosed.

There is also a legal requirement for the rearer to provide a current veterinary prescription for the inclusion of any drugs deemed necessary in order to safeguard the health of birds.

7

The Shooting Day

The shooting day is the culmination of all the hard work carried out during the past rearing season. Careful planning is therefore essential if the shooting season is to run smoothly and successfully.

Although the pheasant shooting season begins on 1 October, it is unusual for shooting to begin seriously until the first weekend in November, when birds will be that little bit stronger and hopefully the trees will have lost some of their leaves. It may be possible to have a couple of fun days in October, especially on ground where partridges have been released and duck flighting can be included at the end of the day. There should be no serious attempt made to get amongst the majority of pheasants on these early days and the drives should consist of a few hedgerows or pieces of rough ground which, if left for the main days, will have been decimated by frosts. Birds dangerously near the boundaries can be shot and others which attempt to fly back to the middle can be left for a later day when they will probably provide a more sporting shot. Never forget that a sporting shot is the objective and the idea is not to kill all the game as quickly as possible.

Julian Tennyson, in *Rough Shooting*, refers to a gentleman shooter whom he met while going to shoot rabbits on his estate near London:

'As it was still September, I asked in some surprise where the partridges were. "In the bag," he told me proudly. "We wiped them up during the first fortnight." '

Only if a pheasant is likely to live on in the mind for several seasons afterwards is it worth shooting.

Planning and Preparation

One of the first things to do when planning a day is to ask about the farmer's plans for certain fields and fences. Once these plans are discovered, the organiser can begin to settle the drives provisionally. If you are only able to visit your shoot weekly in order to fill up the hoppers, it would be of considerable embarrassment to find that a field of kale from which you had planned a drive for the following weekend had suddenly disappeared under a sea of cows. Kale should, by the way, be shot mornings only, as this is the time most favoured by the pheasants.

Even on the smallest shoot, there is always the opportunity to shoot at a driven bird, even though the original intention may have been to keep it as a truly rough shoot and merely walk them up. If the syndicate or guests are split into two teams, they can each take turns in standing and beating. If beaters are to be employed, then their captain or the non-shooting part-time keeper must meet with the shooting team's captain some time before the first day and go around the proposed drives together. On a small shoot there are often too many chiefs and not enough Indians, so whilst all ideas should be considered, do not be tempted into including everyone in this walkabout. Apart from the unnecessary disturbance, not many plans will be made!

Where possible, put out gun pegs so that there can be no confusion as to where people are to stand. Although it may seem a little grand to use these markers when only a couple of dozen birds are expected in the bag at the end of the day, their provision will save much time and shouting. Be prepared to make changes if the wind makes it impossible to drive birds towards these pegs, but otherwise a gun should stand immediately behind his marker until the whistle has been blown to signal the end of the drive. Pegs should be placed about 40m (131ft) apart.

Arrange the drives for the day so that birds are being pushed homewards rather than over the boundary. If one wood or cover can be driven in such a way that it supplies pheasants in another drive, so much the better, but try not to follow on with this drive immediately; birds need a couple of hours to rest and get their strength back before flying again the same day.

Although the sewelling rides and flushing points will have been cut in the early part of the year, they may not have been made by the person who is to be in charge of the beaters and so the pre-shoot walk should be used to point these out and also to think about where 'stops' can be placed to best advantage. As the season progresses, the birds are more likely to run out of the woods when the first shot is fired, rather than sit around waiting to be flushed, and it is often better to put fewer people in the line for the sake of an extra stop or two. Theirs is an important task and they should know exactly what is required of them. In most cases the stop should remain where he is put, tapping his stick gently or even remaining silent unless he sees a bird trying to escape, but he must also know when it pays to move in order to cut off pheasants which he has seen leaking out of another escape route. In another instance, he will need to walk up and down in order to cover a broader front. Like the sewelling person, pick these people carefully and with great thought. Someone who is excitable

A 'stop' at the end of the sewelling. Choose someone reliable who
knows when to tap and when to remain silent.

will probably only succeed in putting birds back over the heads of the beaters.

Plan and prepare every last little detail, right down to the time you expect you will want to stop for lunch. Nearer Christmas, when daylight is short, it may be a good idea to shoot right through lunchtime, although for the small shoot which relies on game covers, a lack of drives may be the deciding factor rather than a lack of light.

Beaters

How many beaters are required will depend on the individual shoot. Your beating team will probably consist of friends and relatives, taking no pay. Please remember that they are out to enjoy themselves. Each drive should be explained to them so that they are not left wondering if they are doing the right thing. When beating woods and game crops for pheasants, the beaters should be in as straight a line as possible and equidistant from each other. In a large wood where beaters are thin on the ground, they may have to zigzag about in order to cover as much ground as possible, so a larger gap then you would ideally like is bound to occur. There should not be too much noise, and most professional keepers and their employers prefer to hear only the sound of sticks tapping – but who can blame a youngster for getting excited when he flushes his first pheasant?

When beating for partridges, the line should be more of a horseshoe shape, and those beaters forming the open ends nearest the guns should carry flags in order to try to turn the birds towards the line of guns. If you decide to do the job properly, permanent hides can be built for the guns along contours which the partridges are most likely to favour. Bales of straw or hessian sacks nailed to a frame will suffice until you are sure that the hides are in exactly the right place. They should be about 40–50m (131–164ft) apart and have been positioned there long enough for the birds to have become used to them.

Picking Up

Very often the small-scale game rearer considers a proper picker-up to be an unnecessary expense but, in my opinion, his wage can easily be paid for by the successful collection of two or three runners which would otherwise go unnoticed and unpicked. Obviously every shooter tries to achieve a clean kill, but it is inevitable that some birds will only be wounded. A person, with a dog, standing well behind the line has more chance of pin-pointing and checking where the bird fell than has the gun who merely

A successful retrieve at the end of the drive. The rough shooter's dog
is as essential a piece of equipment as his gun.

turns, thinks he has missed the bird and looks forward again for another target. Once again, the picker-up should be told exactly where he can or cannot work his dog and, if he is in any doubt, he should check that the collection of a runner will not upset the next drive.

Unlike picking up pheasants, when it is often necessary to stand almost next to the guns, the person picking up partridges needs to stand at least 100m (328ft) behind the line so that pricked birds can be seen. If positioned too close, not only will they distract the guns and put off the partridges, but they will also have further to travel to a fall, and will thus waste valuable time.

Picking up on either a pheasant or partridge shoot should not really be done until the drive is over, but in certain circumstances, such as a very strong runner which the dog has immediately marked, it is only sensible to send the dog straight away and to dispatch the bird as quickly and as humanely as possible. There is no more disgusting a spectacle than seeing a bird being swung against a tree or fence until a hit is scored in the right place. Birds can be dispatched by dislocating the neck (although game dealers do not like to be offered game with broken necks) or, alternatively, a tap with a beating stick is clean and virtually instantaneous. It is not easy to describe the procedure, so I would suggest that the best way of killing wounded stock is learned from someone with experience.

Apart from monies coming in from any syndicate members, it is only on the sale of game that the shoot can make any money. It therefore pays to look after dead game. Even on the small shoot, a properly designed game cart or rack would not be out of place, rather than letting dogs, mud and people fall over the birds in the back of a Landrover. Similarly, the spare tyre on the bonnet of some vehicles is not an ideal place in which to store game. As soon as possible, preferably after each drive, dead birds should be hung in a well ventilated position; any birds which do get wet will soon dry out when hung under cover in a draughty spot.

Shooting after Christmas

Some problems which are likely to occur once the pheasants have got the measure of the shooting days have already been mentioned, but late-season pheasants can provide the true sportsman with some most memorable shooting.

Some shoots put a voluntary ban on hens immediately after Christmas, feeling that a lot of damage can be caused by a general end of season free-for-all when boys' days, beaters' days and fun days are all put in as extra days over and above those already planned. This is only usually applicable when it is intended to catch up hens for breeding, but even when this is carried out it should be possible to catch birds whilst shooting continues.

If the area and ground is suitable, it may pay to go for 'cocks only' towards the end of the season, even when you do not intend to catch up any hens, as this may allow for some natural breeding (provided that predators have been controlled). However, even this is probably only a worthwhile exercise for the very small shoot when wild birds form a vital part of the season's shooting.

Some keepers and shooting people maintain that certain woods are favoured by either cocks or hens, but at the end of a shooting day you will notice that there is not much difference between the numbers of cocks and hens in the final bag. A look at any previous game books will probably show that, throughout the season, a pretty fair balance is achieved.

On the wild bird shoot, too many cocks will result in lower fertility in the breeding stock. Unlike most other species of gamebirds which are monogamous, pheasants are polygamous, so not many cocks are needed. If there are more males than there are territories available, young cocks will be unsuccessful in procuring their own territory and so will spend their time chasing hens which have temporarily wandered from the harem of a more successful mature cock.

An important factor in deciding whether birds breed successfully or not is the availability of suitable nesting sites and food resources. It is these resources that determine population size, rather than the number of birds around. In fact, according to Dr Peter Robinson, Pheasant Study scientist with the Game Conservancy:

'To forbid hen pheasant shooting is a restriction the sport can ill afford, and one which allows a large population of the available game to go to waste.'

Encouraging Reared Ducks to Fly

Reared mallard are notorious for providing a non-event on the shooting day. They must be kept wild, especially when they have been released on a large expanse of water. In such circumstances, small boats can sometimes be used in order to flush mallard which refuse to fly from the middle of the water. Apparently it is against the law to use mechanically propelled boats, so two boats connected by means of a rope can be used to flush the residents quite successfully. If I were a gun, however, I would not be happy to see such methods used and would instead prefer to be present on a shoot where more subtle methods are employed. A flight pond where only a few wild birds are shot is more in tune with the aspirations of the small-scale game rearer and whether or not he gets a shot is incidental.

Some rearers attempt to feed their ducks away from the pond in order to make them fly towards home, but I am sure that any ducks artificially reared and released are better used merely as decoys to encourage any wild birds in the area.

Wild duck are infinitely more wary and the only way to come to terms with them is with the aid of man-made hides. These should be at least 1.5m (4ft 11in) wide by 2m (6ft 6in) long. The height is ideal at about 1.5m (4ft 11in), especially when there is an adjustable fringe attached to the front. This can be made of softwood brashings, or reeds if you are in the right country. A slatted floor (feed and fertiliser pallets make ideal bases) will help to prevent you from creating a mud-bath, as well as keeping a dog off the worst of the wet.

In hard weather, it is often necessary to consider the origins of wild-bred

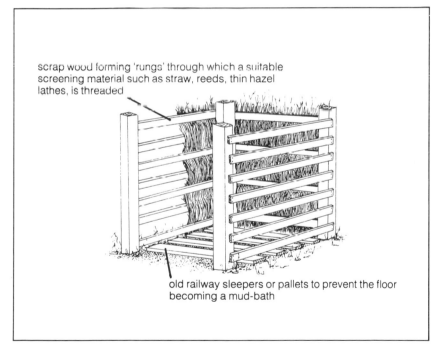

scrap wood forming 'rungs' through which a suitable screening material such as straw, reeds, thin hazel lathes, is threaded

old railway sleepers or pallets to prevent the floor becoming a mud-bath

Before going to the trouble and expense of constructing a permanent duck hide, it may pay to be sure of the correct site by using several hides made from straw bales for one season, in order to be certain of flight lines and the results of local topography.

waterfowl. If they are thought to be having a hard time, it may be prudent for the shoot to impose a voluntary ban on the killing of waterfowl and woodcock. The Nature Conservancy Council, together with the various shooting and conservation organisations, will also get together and advise the relevant government ministers if it is felt that a ban should be made obligatory. The decision will be made public through the national media.

Like pheasants, the duck will have had the opportunity to study the habits of the shooter towards the end of the season, and will tend to flight later than they would in the earlier months of the season. Remember to wait until they are in range. I have seen beaters, given the opportunity to sit around the flight pond on the last day of the season, shoot at birds before they are within gunshot. Patience is indeed a virtue when duck shooting, and shooting too soon only serves to confirm what the ducks half expected when they first circled suspiciously over the pool or lake.

Poaching

Poaching can also affect the affect the season's results, although it must be said that if there is a large shoot in the close vicinity of your rather minor concern, poachers will favour that estate where they can pick up a good quota of birds quickly, and with the least amount of travelling, rather than struggle for a few pheasants on the small acreage.

Large-scale poaching was probably not a serious problem for the keeper until about the 1930s, when cars became common and provided both an easy get-away and a means of transporting ill-gotten gains. There is still a certain amount of roadside poaching being carried out; an air rifle is poked out of the window, a bird is shot and a meal is provided. This in itself is not a great problem, but when the ground also contains vast numbers of deer, there will always be the temptation for poachers to take a carcass and earn more money by doing so than they could by obtaining several brace of pheasants.

Collaboration between neighbouring keepers can help and advanced alarm systems are good, if somewhat expensive, to set up. CB radios probably provide the best answer, as well as proving useful on the shooting day.

Final Points

I have omitted mentioning either records or finances throughout this book. As with any hobby, the small-scale game rearer will only spend what he can afford and should build up his shoot only as far as he can comfortably manage to finance all its aspects.

Where a syndicate situation arises, any bookwork should be carried out by the person understood to be in charge of all shooting matters; he pays all the bills and keeps a book of accounts which should be on a level to satisfy even the most ardent of chartered accountants. Any purchases should be made through this person.

The minimum bookwork that the shooter should undertake is the daily completion of a desk diary. It will provide him with vital information in future years, as well as forming a record of finances from which he can assess the actual cost of his hobby.

Although your shooting day will not compare with some of the large estates up and down the country, it must be just as well organised. If all the arrangements are made well in advance, no one need be aware of them, but one aspect of the day which must never be taken casually is that of gun safety.

If guests are to be invited, some time should be set aside at the start of the day in order to explain to them when, where and what they can shoot. In most cases, a pocket or belt full of cartridges will be enough, but some shoots at the top end of the amateur market may expect the individual to shoot many more cartridges on one of their best days. The guest should be told by his host what he can expect. The ideal host will also explain to his guest whether or not he intends to provide a meal and, if he does, whether it will be served at lunch-time or at the end of the day. If it is to be the end of the day, then the guest will probably be wise to pack a few sandwiches in his pocket.

It is unlikely that the small shoot will need transport to get beaters and guns from one part of the shoot to another, but a four-wheel drive vehicle owned by a shoot member can often be used to great advantage for transporting guns from the meeting place to the first drive. Care must be taken on several counts, however. Too much noise will warn pheasants that all is not well. A light-coloured vehicle parked in the wrong place may turn birds away from the standing guns. Check that the actual owner of the ground will not mind a Landrover running over his ground and tracks.

What has been included in this book has been taken from experience – not just my experience but also that of head keepers under whom I have had the pleasure to work and keepers, both professional and amateur, whom I have met beating or socially – and from books, reports, and the excellent research carried out by the Game Conservancy staff. In learning (and there is something new to be learned every day) there is also a great deal of pleasure to be had and a better understanding of the countryside to be obtained.

The keeper – it does not matter whether he is professional or amateur – is in a better position to conserve the countryside than the average person who, through circumstances, can do no more than feed birds in the back garden. Some people may condemn a few keepering practices but there can be no doubt about the overall benefits of shooting traditions. The small-scale game rearer is not only providing himself with a seasonable day's sport but, much more importantly, is providing his immediate countryside with a better future.

Appendix

Open Seasons

Grouse   12 August–10 December
Pheasant   1 October–1 February
Partridge   1 September–1 February
Woodcock   1 October–31 January
   (Scotland and Ireland   1 September–31 January)
Snipe   12 August–31 January
   (Ireland   1 September–31 January)
Waterfowl   1 September–31 January
   (includes moorhen and coot, except in Northern Ireland and the Irish
   Republic where both moorhen and coot are fully protected)

The Wildlife and Countryside Act, 1981, permits authorised persons to
shoot the following 'pest species' except on Sundays and Christmas Day:

Collared dove	Crow
Wood-pigeon	Starling
Feral pigeon	Sparrow
Magpie	Great and Lesser
Jay	black-backed gull
Herring-gull	Jackdaw

There is no close season for hares, but they may not be killed on Sundays
or Christmas Day. It is, however, illegal to sell hares between 1 March and
31 July.

Useful Addresses

Organisations

The Game Conservancy
Burgate Manor
Fordingbridge
Hampshire

British Association for Shooting
and Conservation
Marford Mill
Chester Road
Rossett
Wrexham
Clwyd

The British Field Sports Society
59 Kennington Road
London SE1

Country Landowners' Association
16 Belgrave Square
London SW1

Forestry Commission
231 Corstorphine Road
Edinburgh EH12

National Ferret Welfare Society
Secretary: A. J. Martin Esq.
56 London Road
Roade
Northampton

Game Farmers' Association
Secretary: S. Jervis-Read Esq.
The Cottage
Little Chart
Ashford
Kent

Kennel Club
1 Clarges Street
London W1

National Farmers Union
Agriculture House
Knightsbridge
London SW1

Sporting Magazines

Countrysport Magazine
Apex House
Vincents Walk
South Street
Dorking
Surrey

The Field
Carmelite House
Carmelite Street
London EC4

Shooting Times
10 Sheet Street
Windsor
Berkshire

Sporting Gun
Bretton Court
Bretton
Peterborough
Cambridgeshire

Dog and Country
Gilbertson and Page
Corrys
Roestock Lane
Colney Heath
St Albans
Hertfordshire

Further Reading

Anderson-Brown, Dr *The Incubation Book* (Saiga Publishing Co. Ltd, 1979)

Bateman, James *Trapping: A Practical Guide*, 5th edition (David & Charles, 1986)

Coles, Charles (editor) *The Complete Book of Game Conservation*, 3rd edition (Hutchinson, 1983)

Forestry Commission *The Wildlife Ranger's Handbook* (Forestry Commission, 1985)

Game Conservancy green booklets:

No. 2 *Game and Shooting Crops*
No. 4 *Partridge Rearing and Releasing*
No. 5 *Pheasant and Partridge Eggs: Production and Incubation*
No. 6 *Diseases of Gamebirds and Wildfowl* (1981)
No. 14 *Feeding and Management of Game in Winter*
No. 22 *Rabbit Control*

Gray, Nigel *Woodland Management for Pheasants and Wildlife* (David & Charles, 1986)

Humphreys, John *Do-it-yourself Game Shoot* (David & Charles, 1985)

Kemp, Michael *A Shoot of Your Own* (A & C Black, 1978)

McCall, Ian *Your Shoot* (A & C Black, 1985)

Moxon, Peter *Gundogs: Training and Field Trials*, 13th edition (Pelham, 1986)

Porter, Val and Brown, Nicholas *The Complete Book of Ferrets* (Pelham, 1985)

Thear, Katie *Practical Chicken Keeping* (Ward Lock, 1983).

Index